Understanding Autism and Autistic Functioning

This concise volume offers an accessible overview of recent clinical and research perspectives addressing autism and autistic functioning. By providing an innovative lens, the book benefits from two different angles: a concrete and pragmatical view of an expert clinician with three decades of practice in diagnosis and treatment of autism, and a more "speculative" and "long-term" view of a researcher who works on neural and computational architecture of (a)typical neurocognitive functioning.

Trying to understand autism beyond its behavioral symptoms, the book spans from clinical descriptions (e.g., communicating diagnosis, clinical intervention, and prognosis) to recent neuroscientific evidence supporting a potential perspective-shift. The *fil rouge* of this volume can be summarized in three fundamental aspects that should orient any clinical practice in the context of autism (e.g., diagnosis, treatment, monitoring, etc.): we need an *age*-dependent, *context*-dependent, and *functioning*-dependent approach.

Understanding Autism and Autistic Functioning is crucial reading for parents and caregivers, and professionals in health, education, and social care.

Laura Villa is a doctor specializing in child neuropsychiatry at the University of Milan (Italy) and also a psychotherapist. She works at the Scientific Institute IRCCS MEDEA – Associazione "La Nostra Famiglia" (Italy), where she is the head of the rehabilitative services for children with autism.

Luca Casartelli is a researcher (PhD from the University of Geneva, Switzerland) and head of the "Theoretical and Cognitive Neuroscience" Research Unit at the Scientific Institute IRCCS MEDEA. Currently, he is also Adjunct Professor of Developmental Neuroscience at Vita-Salute San Raffaele University (Italy) and of Philosophy at the University of Milan (Italy).

Understanding Atypical Development
Series editor: Alessandro Antonietti, Università Cattolica del Sacro Cuore, Italy.

This volume is one of a rapidly developing series in *Understanding Atypical Development*, published by Routledge. This book series is a set of basic, concise guides on various developmental disorders or issues of atypical development. The books are aimed at parents, but also professionals in health, education, social care and related fields, and are focused on providing insights into the aspects of the condition that can be troubling to children, and what can be done about it. Each volume is grounded in scientific theory but with an accessible writing style, making them ideal for a wide variety of audiences.

Each volume in the series is published in hardback, paperback and eBook formats. More information about the series is available on the official website at: www.routledge.com/Understanding-Atypical-Development/book-series/UATYPDEV, including details of all the titles published to date.

Published Titles

Understanding Tourette Syndrome: A Guide to Symptoms, Management and Treatment
By Carlotta Zanaboni Dina and Mauro Porta

Understanding Intellectual Disability: A Guide for Professionals and Parents
By Margherita Orsolini and Ciro Ruggerini

Understanding Autism and Autistic Functioning: A Guide for Parents, Educators and Professionals
Laura Villa and Luca Casartelli

Understanding Autism and Autistic Functioning

A Guide for Parents, Educators and Professionals

Laura Villa and Luca Casartelli

LONDON AND NEW YORK

Cover image: naqiewei via Getty Images

First published 2025
by Routledge
4 Park Square, Milton Park, Abingdon, Oxon OX14 4RN

and by Routledge
605 Third Avenue, New York, NY 10158

Routledge is an imprint of the Taylor & Francis Group, an informa business

© 2025 Laura Villa and Luca Casartelli

The right of Laura Villa and Luca Casartelli to be identified as authors of this work has been asserted in accordance with sections 77 and 78 of the Copyright, Designs and Patents Act 1988.

All rights reserved. No part of this book may be reprinted or reproduced or utilised in any form or by any electronic, mechanical, or other means, now known or hereafter invented, including photocopying and recording, or in any information storage or retrieval system, without permission in writing from the publishers.

Trademark notice: Product or corporate names may be trademarks or registered trademarks, and are used only for identification and explanation without intent to infringe.

British Library Cataloguing-in-Publication Data
A catalogue record for this book is available from the British Library

ISBN: 9780367569693 (hbk)
ISBN: 9780367569723 (pbk)
ISBN: 9781003100140 (ebk)

DOI: 10.4324/9781003100140

Typeset in Sabon
by Newgen Publishing UK

Contents

Series Preface		*vii*
About the Authors		*ix*
	Introduction	1
1	Atypical Preface: Autism and Autistic Functioning LUCA CASARTELLI	3
2	Autism Spectrum Disorder: Insights from a Neuroscientific Perspective LUCA CASARTELLI	21
3	Autism Spectrum Disorder: Communicating Diagnosis LAURA VILLA	42
4	Autism Spectrum Disorder: Clinical Intervention and Treatment LAURA VILLA	62
5	Autism Spectrum Disorder: Positive Prognosis, Optimal Outcome, Best *Feasible* Outcome, and Recovery LAURA VILLA	103
	Conclusive Considerations	120
	Index	122

Series Preface

Statistical data supports the notion that the incidence of developmental disorders, and more generally the presence of atypical behaviors in childhood and youth, is increasing in the population around the world. This does not necessarily depend on the fact that pathological conditions are wide-spreading; it might be the outcome of increased interest toward the conditions of children and adolescents, greater diffusion of knowledge about the features of atypical development, or higher levels of sophistication and implementation that diagnostic procedures have reached. In any case, adults who have to support and drive the growth of the younger generations are challenged to find effective ways to manage situations which require special attention. Specialists who take care of children and adolescents with special needs can do a part of this work. But another part is the responsibility of people who live with those children and adolescents, and interact with them outside the therapeutic setting. The contribution of parents, teachers, and trainers in extra-school domains (such as sport, art, hobbies, edutainment, religious education, and social activities) can be relevant. These people should be knowledgeable about the effective ways of communicating, engaging, instructing, monitoring, and tutoring atypically developing children and adolescents in order to support their growth efficiently. This book series tries to fit this need.

The series aims to be a set of basic, concise guides on various developmental disorders or issues of atypical development. The books provide insights into the aspects of the condition that can be troubling to children and adolescents and what can be done about them. Each volume follows a basic structure and is grounded in scientific theory but written very accessibly for the target audience. Typically, each book faces the following issues:

- Signs and symptoms of the disorder
- What causes the disorder
- Available treatments and therapies
- Living with the condition
- Practical ways to help children with the disorder and to support caregivers
- Communicating the diagnosis to peers
- Cultural differences and sensitivities.

The series is written for parents, caregivers, and professionals, with particular emphasis on health, social care, and education. The books are of value to practitioners in clinical and educational psychology, counselling, mental health, nursing, teacher training, child welfare, social work, and youth work as well. Professionals and trainees involved in relevant medical disciplines – including midwives, health visitors, school nursing, and public health professionals – and those in general practice, as well as those involved in education including teachers, classroom assistants and all those concerned with Early Years can benefit from the books.

Alessandro Antonietti
Department of Psychology –
Catholic University of the Sacred Heart
Milan, Italy
Editor of the series *Understanding Atypical Development*

About the Authors

Laura Villa is a doctor specializing in child neuropsychiatry (University of Milan, Italy) and also a psychotherapist. She works at the Scientific Institute IRCCS MEDEA – Associazione "La Nostra Famiglia" (Italy), where she is chief of the rehabilitative services for children with autism. As a child neuropsychiatrist, she has decades of clinical experience in early diagnosis and early differential diagnosis of neurodevelopmental disorders. Scientific Institute IRCCS MEDEA – Associazione "La Nostra Famiglia" is both a pediatric research hospital specialized in developmental clinical neuroscience and a rehabilitative center with 28 branches in 6 regions in Italy.

She is an invited professor in several postgraduate national master's programs, and also a clinical supervisor for many national services for autism. She collaborates with several research units of the Scientific Institute IRCCS MEDEA for clinical studies, focusing on monitoring of atypical developmental trajectories in autism, early detection and early diagnosis of autism, and more generally neurobiology of autism.

Luca Casartelli has a background in disciplines ranging from philosophy to neuroscience, and he studied in Italy (University of Milan and Politecnico di Milano), France (Jean-Moulin LYON3 University and University of Strasbourg), and Switzerland (University of Geneva, for his PhD). He is the principal investigator of the "Theoretical and Cognitive Neuroscience" Research Unit at the Scientific Institute IRCCS MEDEA (Italy), a pediatric research hospital specialized in developmental clinical neuroscience. Currently, he is Adjunct Professor of Developmental Neuroscience at Vita-Salute San Raffaele University and

Philosophy at the University of Milan, Italy. In 2023, he has been Associate Research Fellow at the Italian Institute of Technology (Center for Human Technology). His research mainly focuses on modeling of motor cognition and (multi)sensory processing both in nonclinical and clinical populations, notably in autism and cerebellar-related disturbances. Among others, his studies have been published in high-impact scientific journals such as *PNAS*, *Neuroscience and Biobehavioral Reviews*, *Physics of Life Reviews*, *Neuroimage*, and *Cerebral Cortex*.

Introduction

The term "autism" raises a myriad of contrasting replies, feelings, reactions, and concerns.

We are aware that it would be impossible to tackle all of them in a single book. We are also aware that – in the context of autism – we probably have more questions than answers. We know that we have not definitive or miraculous solutions. Nevertheless, we are aware that we cannot be indifferent to challenges that individuals with a diagnosis of autism and their families have to deal with.

Here, we try to benefit from two distinct "lens" for promoting a better understanding of autism and the autistic functioning. From one side, we have the concrete and pragmatical view of an expert clinician with three decades of practice in diagnosis and treatment of autism (Laura Villa); from the other side, there is the more speculative and "long-term" view of a researcher who works on theoretical, cognitive, and clinical neuroscience (Luca Casartelli). These views may sometimes appear very distant and detached. However, we strongly believe that they should interact and cooperate more strictly.

Structure of the book

This book is organized into five chapters. First, in the so-called "Atypical Preface" (Chapter 1), Luca Casartelli proposes a specific point of view that tries to "deconstruct" classical approaches on autism grounded primarily – or even exclusively – on behavioral symptoms (e.g., social difficulties, repetitive behaviors, and restricted interests), and he draws a specific (maybe more challenging) view focused on the construct of "autistic functioning".

In Chapter 2, Luca Casartelli proposes a critical (and concise) picture of recent neuroscientific findings in the context of autism. This chapter should not be considered as a comprehensive or systematic review for clinicians and researchers (many valuable works are already available in the literature). This chapter should promote the understanding of the potential value of research for individuals with autism, without neither overestimating nor underestimating its impact.

In Chapter 3, Laura Villa focuses on the crucial phases of the communication of the diagnosis. These phases may unavoidably entail difficulties and concerns, but they should be also considered in light of the proactive cascade effects that can trigger.

In Chapter 4, Laura Villa considers the ample, multifaceted scenario of treatment in the context of autism. It would be not only unrealistic but probably also misleading to describe *any* treatment or *any* hypothetical approach. The focus will be on evidence-based treatments and their methodological framework.

Finally, in Chapter 5 Laura Villa tackles the delicate issue related to potential outcomes after having received a diagnosis of autism. Positive prognosis, optimal outcome, best *feasible* outcome, and recovery are constructs that will be considered and critically analyzed.

We did our best to be scientifically rigorous, and at the same time we tried to be clear for readers without specific clinical or research background. We also did our best in using terms, expressions, and constructs to be as fair and supportive as possible for individuals with autism (and for their families, etc.). We apologize for possible concepts or phrases – if any – that can be appeared to someone unsuitable or unfair.

No doubts that this book will not clarify *any* doubts or *any* misinterpretations in the context of autism. However, we hope that it may be useful to make a step forward – notably for general readers – in understanding autism and the autistic functioning.

Chapter 1

Atypical Preface
Autism and Autistic Functioning

Luca Casartelli

Autism: what it is and what it is not

Autism is not a rare disease, and it is not even a disease. Autism is a lifelong neurodevelopmental condition impacting in atypical and heterogeneous ways the social and communicative abilities, interests, and often the daily life activities of individuals. Although how complex brain mechanisms contribute to behavioural manifestations of the condition is far to be fully clarified, nowadays it is largely demonstrated that autism spectrum disorder (ASD) has relevant neurobiological counterpart, including a genetic one shaped by gene and environment interplay. Recent epidemiological research agrees in reporting a significant increase in ASD prevalence, but differences exist between samples from distinct areas (e.g., low-income countries and high-income ones, in which formal diagnosis rate is even higher) (Lai et al., 2020). Nevertheless, global increase in the number of ASD diagnoses is undeniable also beyond differences primarily driven by socio-economic factors. Increased public awareness of developmental age, importance and attentiveness on neurodevelopmental disorders, improvements in recognizing autistic manifestations (even in cases in which they are subtle), and refinement in diagnostic criteria are surely the most evident components contributing to the evolution of ASD as a categorical construct, and in turn to its increased prevalence (Rosen et al., 2021). This does not exclude *a priori* that also other biological or environmental risk factors may have played a role in this increase, but only future rigorous research will be able to clarify their potential contribution. To underline the need of reliable research is not only a generic reference to a widely shared contemporary "pro-science mantra", but it is also an urgent call for a responsible and prudent communication, especially in very sensitive domains such as autism. Clinicians and researchers worldwide, the scientific community in general, caregivers and politicians should be aware that vague, rough or even misleading statements concerning autism (in terms of potential causes or putative treatment) may have dreadful effects on people that may not master neurobiology or complex scientific methodologies. Recent events, from earthquake forecasting to pandemic management, strongly invite all people to fix their attention to the "real" value of scientific data, and notably the "probabilistic" sense of scientific findings. This should not undermine the central role that scientific advancement can have in supporting and driving decisions in public health as well as in clinical context. Science is a promising and astonishing endeavour, and clinicians and researchers should be personally and morally engaged with it. To recognize that science may also run into misinterpretation, mistake and even fraudulent deceit does not mean that reliable, rigorous and insightful scientific data are just an exception. *Au contraire*, most clinicians and researchers have strong and passionate faith in the scientific progress, including progress in understanding and treating autism. We have to accept the complexity and the *in progress* nature of scientific endeavour, without underestimating potentiality and risks of this astonishing challenge. Thus, it is necessary to be clear and unambiguous: this book neither unveils a "secret cause" of autism nor a "miraculous treatment" for autism, because we simply do not have them (and very probably they literally do not exist, at least in these terms). Declaring confidence in rigorous clinical and scientific approaches, this chapter tries to combine scientific evidence with a sort of narrative and behavioural based analysis of the *autistic functioning*. We aim to focus on autism to shed light on the autistic functioning, being aware that an in-depth understanding of this peculiar functioning can promote a beneficial snowball effect in a wide spectrum of domains, ranging from early intervention to public health policies. Here again, we do not have miraculous solutions, and we do not reveal hidden truths. Benefiting from the state-of-the-art, evidence-based clinical and scientific knowledge we try to draw a picture that may help to do at least one step forward for individuals with ASD,[1] for parents, for teachers, for caregivers and, ultimately, for the society.

Autism is a neurodevelopmental condition with age-dependent phenotypical manifestations

In the past few decades, an impressive body of studies has largely improved our understanding of autism, and these efforts converge in ascertaining that autism is an *early* emerging condition. In turn, this implies that we should promote *early* diagnosis and *early* intervention to maximize positive outcomes (Klin et al., 2020). How this emphasis on timely care has been effectively translated in diagnostic and rehabilitative processes is obviously strongly influenced by the specific characteristics of each national health system, and their detailed synthesis would represent a titanic work. We do not intend to pursue this aim, here. We do not neither focus on significant ethical challenges posed by early detection of ASD, although they represent an important and often underestimated aspect. For example, we should consider the balance of risks and benefits of early identification not only in light of false positive or false negative cases, but also in light of potential comorbidities with other neurodevelopmental conditions that may result in complex clinical pictures. In turn, clinicians need robust and appropriate skills for communicating early concerns to families according to not only the best of their scientific knowledge concerning the clinical picture, but also in a way that fits with the specific contextual and familiar situation. Here, beyond these important aspects that will receive further attention in the book, we would like to take into account this emphasis stressing the need of considering early diagnosis and early intervention next to the idea that autism is a neuro*developmental* condition, that is, it presents distinct phenotypical manifestations across development. Accordingly, the idea of *age-dependent* approach to autism represents one of the key tips that should be preserved. Here, we do not refer to the triviality that toddlers and adolescents with ASD may have distinct needs in terms of rehabilitative, psychological, or educational support. Indeed, it is crucial to point the age-dependent phenotypical manifestation of the autistic functioning. This means that clinicians, and more generally caregivers, should consider that "classical" core domains of ASD (e.g., socio-communicative abilities, repetitive behaviours, restricted interests, etc.) are not static and immutable boxes, whereas they are umbrella terms for referring to *in progress* and age-dependent set of phenotypical manifestations. The fact that these labels may be refined in time according to scientific and clinical progress does not undermine their usefulness. More simply, and here again, this drives us to be suspicious of simplistic solutions. Let us take an example. A growing body of evidence ascertains the critical role of sensory and perceptual peculiarities in autism, notably early derailments in sensory/perceptual developmental trajectories may trigger cascade effects impacting higher (e.g., social) functioning (Robertson and Baron-Cohen, 2017). Clinicians and researchers agree, and caregivers widely confirm, that hypersensibility to acoustic stimuli may strongly impact one's ability to manage social interactions in noisy environment. Suppose that you are facing a 10-year-old child with ASD in a candy shop while a very kind shop assistant helps him in choosing his favourite sweets, and suddenly he runs away from the candy shop hurting people and crying. Is it "just" a socio-communicative problem or the socio-communicative difficulty should be considered the snowball effect of sensory hypersensitivity (maybe due to the entrance of a loud and jubilant group of local football team supporters)? Analysing this very simplistic and trivial example, one cannot deny the "social" component (i.e., to run away hurting people and crying is generally not a suitable reaction); at the same time, limiting the focus to such an aspect would prevent our understanding of the factors leading to this behaviour (i.e., hyper-responsiveness to auditory stimulation). And what about a 3-year-old child with ASD that does not play with her classmates at the kindergarten, whereas she prefers to stay alone looking at the swing? The "final" effect of her behaviour would probably be labelled as "social difficulty", but what about the reasons? Is she "simply" avoiding too noisy games with other children? Is she "simply" attracted by swing rhythmic oscillatory pattern? Is the combination of noise-aversion and rhythmic movement-attraction the key factor driving her behaviour? And what about a 30-year-old individual with ASD refusing a date to avoid crossing the confusing street market? Is it "social" reluctance? These simplistic and imaginary examples describe age-dependent consequences of sensory hypersensitivity, with clear impact on the ability to promote social interactions. Noteworthy, the behavioural analysis of these illustrative conducts does not suggest any sort of "social reluctance", whereas it seems to indicate a different sensitivity to sensory stimulation whose cascade effect impacts (negatively) the social functioning. Thus, these examples not only indicate that the impact of autism on individuals evolves over time, but they also suggest thought-provoking considerations concerning the presumed primary position of the social-communicative domain in autism. Maybe we should go even more directly to the point. Is ASD just the categorical label used to refer to a heterogeneous set of phenotypical manifestations including socio-communicative difficulties, restricted and repetitive patterns of behaviours? Should we consider ASD diagnosis as the completion of a behavioural checklist? Is it enough to understand, and hopefully support, individuals with ASD? We suspect that it is not enough.

Focus on the autistic functioning

On the one hand, autism is a medical condition requiring appropriate differential diagnosis and the evaluation of potential comorbidities (e.g., epilepsy, sleep disorders, etc.). In these terms, autism can be considered as a disability that requires treatment and intervention. On the other hand, each individual with ASD manifests a profile of strengths, differences, weaknesses, and peculiarities that constitute the core of his/her functioning. Beyond inter-individual variability and non-negligible heterogeneity, the term *autistic functioning* may profitably serve to shed light on this second aspect. Is there a diagnostic test or quantitative marker to fix this idea of autistic functioning? Unfortunately, no. Should we consider it as the "resolutive solution" for diagnosing and treating autism? Probably, no. May it be useful to improve our understanding of autistic behavioural manifestations and, in turn, to propose even more timely detection, refined rehabilitation, and to promote social interactions? We think so. By now, we have just "images" and "qualitative descriptions" (ideally grounded on experimental findings) to characterize this idea. Conjugating these descriptions, we should be able to draw a clearer picture of this idea, although prudence is essential to avoid oversimplification. Notably, it is important to avoid drawing a too rigid "model" of the autistic functioning that would not fit with the well-recognized (by clinicians, by researchers, and primarily by caregivers) heterogeneity of phenotypical manifestations. Let us present some of these "images" or "qualitative descriptions" that refer to idea of autistic functioning.

Autistic functioning seems to be characterized by *processing differences more than resemblances*. What does it mean? When neurotypical individuals find a set of crayons in the pencil, usually they tend to ideally group them according to one of their common features (e.g., they are wooden tools useful for drawing and especially appreciated by children and artists; they constitute the "school-starting pack" for my 6-year-old son; etc.). In turn, neurotypical individuals have generally no troubles in replying to this common request: "Please, can you loan me something for drawing?". They simply pass *a* crayon, having generalized the functional meaning of each crayon as they had a sort of "common denominator" (i.e., to be tools for drawing). Computationally, this generalization seems to be characterized by the inclination to look for similarities and shared properties. In contrast, it happens that the autistic functioning tends to focus on *this* crayon, the green one placed in the pencil case on the table at Tom's school. To some extent, it seems that Tom does not see *a* crayon, whereas he sees a number of specific, well-characterized crayons (i.e., the green one, the red one, the blue one, etc.). Moreover, even the green crayon *is not the same* when it is used at school or at home, if it is in the pencil case or accidentally fallen on the floor, if it is used to draw the school garden or courgettes, if it is used to draw or to write Tom's name. Maybe, we can even say that Tom is seeing only "hyper-characterized" crayons, or a collection of very specific, rigid, fixed, and immutable crayons. Here, we need to be honest. Is Tom's approach meaningless or totally illogical? Absolutely, no. Maybe, it could be considered even a more logical approach. It is undeniable that the green crayon is different from the red one if we focus on the "colour" property. It is undeniable that the green crayon used at school is different from the one used at home if we focus on the spatio-temporal localization of the crayon. So, which is the point? The point is that most times we simply need *a* crayon, and processing similarities instead of differences is usually more efficient. In addition, most people refer to *a* crayon, and not to *the green one placed in the pencil case at Tom's school*. This means that most people may consider "weird" the Tom's very detailed, hyper-specified requests ("Which one? The green one placed in my pencil case on my desk at school?). Tom's reply is not wrong *per se*, it is "simply" not parsimonious. Notably, it is not a singular "weird" request that undermines effective social dynamic, whereas it is the recurring use of this atypical functioning (i.e., the propensity to process differences instead of resemblances) that can impact – with a snowball effect – on the effectiveness of social dynamics. May the tendency of processing differences instead of resemblances be the cause or fully explain autism? Obviously, no.

Autistic functioning may be also described as a peculiar cognitive style characterized by *intolerance of uncertainty and "black and white thinking"*, which refers to the tendency of thinking in absolutes and dichotomies without "grey zone" (Stark et al., 2021). Beyond our intimate beliefs, what we perceive depends heavily on a set of "expectations" (see also the construct of "predictive brain", Yon et al., 2018) from which we build a probabilistic representation of the world. Thus, what we expect to hear or see interferes with, and even supersedes, what we actually hear and see. Similarly, when we produce and perform actions, we also predict their likely consequences. Notably, we are largely unaware of these expectations and predictions. What we see or hear is just a "balanced synergy" of sensory inputs and (largely unaware) predictions concerning what we expect to see or hear (Clark, 2013; Press et al., 2020). This tainted access to reality is not unreasonable. Having expectations about the world is a tool to predict the future and, in turn, to promote fluent social dynamics. Recent studies in the literature hypothesized that in autism incoming sensory signals are weighted differently when they are integrated with the brain's existing model of the environment, with cascade effects impacting the way in which individuals with ASD reply to these stimuli (Van de Cruys et al., 2014; Palmer et al., 2017). More simply, in autism the "balanced synergy" between incoming sensory stimulation and predictions seems to follow different rules compared to neurotypical individuals. In turn, the interplay among atypical predictive processing, intolerance of uncertainty, and "black and white thinking" has been suggested to result in the peculiar autistic cognitive style that seems to be less incline to manage the intrinsic instability of the environment; in turn, the autistic functioning would tend to prefer highly predictable situations instead of "grey zones". How many combinations of factors drive my (visual, auditory, or olfactory) perception of that open-air market? How less predictable is it compared to my kitchen? How changeable are these factors driven by physical (e.g., light) and non-physical elements (e.g., my previous personal experience of this kitchen)? Can we limit the instability of the environment fixing lights, noises, and odours in a rigid way? Here again, the peculiar way in which individuals with ASD seem to be prone to deal with the environment (i.e., their peculiar interplay between expectations and incoming sensory stimuli) is not wrong *per se*. More properly, we should say that the autistic functioning seems to be less efficient in replying to the common degree of instability of our environment. It is *de facto* less efficient, in the sense that most people (neurotypical ones) interact profitably with the environment, whereas individuals with ASD often show troubles in managing it.

A further somehow convergent view proposes *inflexibility of thinking, of acting, and primarily of learning (or habit of sameness)* as key features of the autistic functioning, making reference both to clinical and experimental studies (Casartelli et al., 2018a; see also Mercado et al., 2020). This view focuses on the dynamic between stability and flexibility, and notably on the ability of proceeding in a stable manner under fixed conditions, while rapid and efficient changes are provided in case of contingent physical or contextual variations. How this dynamic between stability and flexibility in a wide range of domains is supported and promoted in neurotypical and autistic functioning remains a matter of research, although one may hypothesize distinct rules in regulating this dynamic between individuals with ASD and neurotypical individuals.

We have briefly introduced the idea that distinct rules in processing, sampling, and categorizing stimuli and, more generally, in managing cognitive processing may have cascade effects on driving behaviours, and this should be considered a key point to understand the autistic functioning. Among these distinct rules, a further recent perspective suggests that in certain cases the autistic functioning seems to exhibit *"bias-free decision-making"* compared to the one exhibited by neurotypical individuals (Rozenkrantz et al., 2021). Evidence from a range of disciplines hypothesizes that neurotypical individuals are characterized by the tendency of processing information in a biased manner, and significant cognitive biases seem to impact their "pure" rational behaviours. Evolutionarily, this "irrational" tendency has been demonstrated to be beneficial in managing a number of daily life situations, as if neglecting some details may promote more parsimonious approaches to complex circumstances. This is linked to seminal works theorizing that humans use cognitive shortcuts, or heuristics, to limit cognitive load during decision-making and judgements (Tversky and Kahneman, 1974). They suggested that the heuristics was adaptive because it permits to reach a decision without fully processing every single information, in turn speeding up the results and optimizing cognitive resources. Obviously, heuristics has also some costs: they are not infallible. This means that humans generally benefit from shortcuts, but sometimes they are deceived by their own optimization strategies. Here again, the autistic functioning seems to rely on a rational schema, or even a more rational than the neurotypical individuals' one. It is a schema in which susceptibility to elements that normally confound rational thought and behaviour seems to be reduced. Maybe this more rational schema is not (often/usually) beneficial, but this view strongly supports the idea that in autism we are not facing an absence of schema or a "broken" schema. In contrast, autistic functioning seems to rely on a different schema compared to neurotypical individuals that, in most cases, use an approximative and/but parsimonious schema. How this autistic cognitive style represents a specific trait or how it is shared also by other clinical conditions is a matter of debate. However, it remains a further peculiar description that may help to characterize the idea of autistic functioning.

Deconstructing the monolithic view of social cognition focusing on its multilayered architecture

Images and qualitative descriptions have the merit of providing hints to sketch the idea of autistic functioning. However, none of them really and fully catches this multifaceted idea. Probably there is not a way to fully catch it. Anyone that deals with individuals with ASD very likely has recognized familiar traits in these descriptions; however, we suspect that many clinicians and researchers may have been surprised by the relatively limited centrality of the social domain in this "Atypical Preface". Notably, no reference to notions such as "theory of mind" or their cognate terms such as "mindreading" and "mentalizing" has been provided. This absence may be unexpected considering that their usage has been massive in the last few decades in the context of autism, reflecting the dominant role of "theory of mind" hypothesis in the literature to explain social cognition. Here, we focus on this somehow unexpected point because implications are remarkable both theoretically and clinically. The original use of the term "theory of mind" referred to the ability of inferring others' mental states, which include beliefs, desires, or intentions. In turn, presumed "theory of mind" deficit was attributed to certain clinical conditions, notably autism. Although such an approach had the merit of acknowledging a self-evident feature of autism (i.e., recurrent and marked difficulties in social dynamics), we suspect that its direct translation in experimental terms may have been simplistic and somehow misleading. In the mainstream literature on autism, a number of studies have tried to demonstrate that "theory of mind" does not work in individuals with ASD as in neurotypical individuals. According to the experimental techniques employed, from behavioural studies to functional magnetic resonance imaging (fMRI) ones, scholars hypothesized presumed deficit in the "mentalizing" system or impairment of the "social brain" network in autism (Elsabbagh and Johnson, 2016). Beyond the widely shared and often simplistic support to these views in the literature, mixed and inconsistent findings characterize this topic. Probably the major source of confusion arises because many publications implicitly treat "theory of mind" as a monolithic process that refers to a presumed well-defined brain network. In contrast, an in-depth analysis of this construct clearly ascertains that varieties of components, functions, and mechanisms have been conflated in the "theory of mind" construct, making weak its readability and usefulness in operational terms (i.e., the reliability of experimental approaches for testing the so-called "theory of mind" is scarce). For example, a prominent distinction can be made between a rapid, automatic form of "theory of mind" largely independent by verbal competence (implicit "theory of mind") and a slower, deliberative form of "theory of mind" characterized by metacognitive efforts. Exploring the last two decades of literature concerning "theory of mind" and autism, it seems that scholars have different concepts in mind when they investigate this notion, even if they pursue in using the same term. Thus, beyond folk psychology agreement about the fact that humans (and even many other animals) have competences in making sense of the observed behaviours of others, how to exactly quantify and test these competences remains largely unclarified. The notion itself appears quite vague. In turn, it remains even more nebulous the hypothetical demonstration of "theory of mind" deficit in autism. Recent refined approaches argue that multilayered notions such as "mindreading", "mentalizing" and "theory of mind" should be deconstructed into more basic components to be profitably explored and quantified (Schaafasma et al., 2014). We should disentangle the contribution of distinct functions and computations to provide testable processes that may be considered a proxy of social cognition, and in turn test putative difficulties in these processes in clinical conditions. Although a refined approach deconstructing the "theory of mind" concept may significantly improve our understanding of social domain in autism, we suspect that it is not enough. We also need a refined idea of social cognition and social functioning.

Classically, social functioning is considered a taken-for-granted phenomenon that, in certain clinical disorders including autism, is somehow limited and problematic. However, an in-depth analysis can easily ascertain that social dynamic is complex and multifaceted experience. Recognizing this complexity is not without consequences. For example, if we suppose that (complex and multifaceted) social dynamics have specialized neural resources, then we should hypothesize something like a "social brain" phylogenetically and ontogenetically set for supporting the complexity of social experience. In contrast, if we hypothesize that (complex and multifaceted) social dynamics share neural resources also with other "non-social" cognitive, perceptual, and motor functions, then the complexity of social dynamics should necessarily be deconstructed into more basic (sub)computations that interchange their activities with other functions. In other words, we should disambiguate whether social conducts are supported by neural structures and processes specifically dedicated to "social" aims ("social brain" hypothesis) or, in contrast, domain-general functions and unspecific neural processes support *also* social functions. Recent neuroscience evidence does not find any clear proof of the existence of a special "social box" in the brain, whereas they seem to be more consistent with the second view that implies the overcoming (or at least the re-definition) of the "social brain" hypothesis (Lockwood et al., 2020). A further intriguing consideration may arise from a recent work by Deschrijver and Palmer (2020). They suggest that classical approaches to social cognition are grounded on the premise that social ability reflects one's sensitivity in efficiently inferring others' thoughts, beliefs, and feelings (as synthetized by the "theory of mind" hypothesis). However, according to the authors, classical approaches neglect a further critical aspect. Indeed, we not only infer others' mental states, but also continuously monitor the extent to which a represented mental state of another person is matching or mismatching with our own (Deschrijver and Palmer, 2020). This aspect has been referred to as "mental conflict monitoring", and it has been proposed to reframe previous literature on "theory of mind hypothesis", taking into account the role of (mis)matching between mental processes. We praise this insight, and we agree in claiming that this point may be pivotal for understanding social dynamic. In social interactions it is not only crucial to catch others' mental state, but also crucial to be sensitive to the extent that others share my own understanding of the world. Thus, the authors suggest that for promoting efficient social dynamic we need not only to compute what others think, but we also need to understand when others think differently. Such a reframing may trigger new considerations also in the context of autism, leading to an alternative (but not necessarily mutually exclusive) view compared to the classical "theory of mind" deficit hypothesis. What about the possibility that individuals with ASD do not show difficulties in grasping *what* others think, whereas they may experience more subtle issues in monitoring potential conflicts between their own and others' mental states? What about the possibility that individuals with ASD, as suggested by Deschrijver and Palmer (2020), may experience troubles when they monitor *the extent to which others are thinking differently from themselves*? Although to date we do not have extended research supporting experimentally and clinically this view, it seems a promising perspective being able to reconnect certain aspects that emerged in this "Atypical Preface". For example, the hypothesis that social cognition should be characterized not only starting from the ability to catch others' mental states (classical "theory of mind" hypothesis), but also from the propensity of revealing conflicts between my and others' thoughts nicely fits with the idea that individuals with ASD do not see *a* crayon. Accordingly, one may hypothesize that Tom sees the conflict between *a* crayon and his *green crayon placed in the pencil case at school*. Future research should clarify how this speculative hypothesis is also testable and empirically supported by clinical and experimental findings. Nevertheless, it surely contributes to a deeper understanding of the nuances of the autistic functioning, keeping constant the attention on the subtle and underestimated *differences* that – with cascade effect – contribute to the heterogeneous phenotypical manifestations of autism.

A further perspective-shift in the autism literature has recently been proposed for the social cognition domain. It is focused on the idea that promoting social dynamic is not only crucial to understand how others think and feel, but also crucial to make others understand us. Although intuitively unsurprising, the bidirectionality of social dynamic has been basically neglected by researchers, and probably naively taken-for-granted by clinicians. Recognizing that difficulties in social interaction for individuals with ASD could result from the failings of both ASD and neurotypical individuals in understanding each other may open new and underestimated issues. First, we may balance the unidirectional search of putative ASD individuals' "deficit" in understanding others. This does not intend to simply overturn the perspective, as we meant to share the "burden" of this inefficient social dynamic "charging" both ASD and neurotypical individuals of any kind of "deficit". There is not a "burden" to be disclosed. In contrast, this bidirectional approach would promote a more genuine analysis of social dynamics, and in turn may inspire a more efficient (rehabilitative) approach to potential intervention. Inefficient communicative dynamics should be overcome by promoting the mutual interaction between neurotypical and ASD individuals. This means that – *a priori* – neurotypical and ASD individuals should try to improve both their understanding of others and the "readability" of their behaviours by others. How much such an endeavour is challenging should not be underestimated, and here again we have not easy and ready-to-use solutions. Intriguingly, a recent perspective coming from neuroscience literature nicely fits with the idea of bidirectionality of the social dynamic. A growing body of evidence hypothesizes the existence of neural circuits supporting the so-called "action execution–action observation" network, that is, our brain elicits comparable activations when we grasp a glass to drink, and when we observe someone else grasping a glass to drink. In other words, there is a "neural matching" between the *motor representations* of a specific action goal (to-grasp-a-glass-for-drinking) when the action is executed or simply observed (or even imagined, or even when the specific action goal is recalled through the correspondent sound) (Rizzolatti and Sinigaglia, 2016). This led to propose the notion of "motor resonance" referring to a set of brain structures supporting (motor) matching mechanisms driven by the "meaning" of action (e.g., to drink; to eat; etc.). In turn, motor resonance is supposed to play a critical "social" role promoting a sort of "motor understanding" of other's action. This implies that we can access to others' mind not only through a metacognitive route, but also via a direct, motor-mediated, "from the inside" route (Rizzolatti and Sinigaglia, 2010). What does concretely it mean? It means that social cognition is not a monolithic process, and the routes through which we can understand other's behaviours are multiple (and mutually non-exclusive).

Here, it is an example of the metacognitive route: "I am noticing that Jack is speaking for 2 hours; in addition, it is a boiling summer, and the air-conditioning is broken; he is raising his arm to the water glass; I think he is going to drink". Conversely, the second route is much more "basic" and "automatic", and it is mediated by motor resonance; it refers to the fact that my brain "catches" the meaning of Jack's arm movement (i.e., to drink) activating the same circuits that it would activate if I grasp the glass to drink (first-person action). More simply, I am "motorically" understanding Jack's action simply eliciting the same "motor" representation that I would elicit if I personally perform that action. To be more poetical, expert tennis players better (and more deeply) understand the magical Jannik Sinner's forehand point because they understand it also "motorically" (in contrast, they very probably lack to understand "motorically" the likewise magical Tiger Woods' golf swing, except that they were also expert golf player). The perspective-shift provided by the study of mirror mechanisms represents one of the most intriguing developments in neuroscience of the last few decades not only for its importance in basic research, but also for the widespread clinical implications of this discovery. Setting apart initial simplistic assumptions naively reported in the literature that proposed a sort of "broken mirror system" hypothesis for autism, as anticipated above more refined approaches to "action execution–action observation" matching mechanisms may not only support the idea of bidirectionality of social dynamic, but also – and more generally – provide interesting insights into the role of "high-level" motor components in autism (Casartelli et al., 2016). In other words, recent and convergent studies provide evidence that non-motor consequences, and notably "social" ones, may derive from anomalies in setting and regulating "action execution–action observation" matching (or, more technically, from anomalies in motor representation mechanisms at distinct levels of the motor hierarchy, see Casartelli et al., 2018b). This strongly supports the idea that social dynamic is a complex and multifaceted phenomenon, and the metacognitive level (and its cognate definitions, such as "mindreading" or "theory of mind" system) is *one* of these levels. Motor cognition supported by motor resonance mechanisms would be the second one. Even more basic levels, such as the ones mediated by sensory and perceptual processing, have been proposed in the literature. Taken together, distinct and non-mutually exclusive levels of social functioning strongly suggest that social cognition is a complex phenomenon. In turn, approaching social functioning in autism neglecting its multilayered nature would undermine the possibility of drawing a reliable picture of putative autistic individuals' difficulties. Here again, we refuse simplistic explanations, and we anticipate that we have not magical solutions. Here, we would like to stress the need of challenging this complexity.

Note

1 A recent debate focused on the use of person-first language (i.e., "individual with ASD") and identity-first language (i.e., "autistic people"). Here, we cannot deal in detail with this debate although we recognize the importance of each argumentation. Practical reasons oblige to choose between one of these alternative uses, and we also did it for this book alternating the options as they were interchangeable. We hope this choice can be understood by everyone, and we obviously remark that we respect any individual preference on this topic.

References

Casartelli, L., Molteni, M., & Ronconi, L. (2016). Neuroscience and biobehavioral reviews so close yet so far: Motor anomalies impacting on social functioning in autism spectrum disorder. *Neuroscience and Biobehavioral Reviews*, 63, 98–105.

Casartelli, L, Riva M, Villa L., & Borgatti, R. (2018a). Insights from perceptual, sensory, and motor functioning in autism and cerebellar primary disturbances: Are they reliable markers for these disorders? *Neuroscience and Biobehavioral Reviews*, 95, 263–279.

Casartelli, L., Federici, A., Biffi, E., Molteni, M., & Ronconi, L. (2018b). Are we "motorically" wired to others? High-level motor computations and their role in autism. *Neuroscientist*. 24(6), 568–581.

Clark, A. (2013). Whatever next? Predictive brains, situated agents, and the future of cognitive science. *Behavioral and Brain Sciences*, 36(3), 181–204.

Deschrijver, E., & Palmer, C. (2020). Reframing social cognition: Relational versus representational mentalizing. *Psychological Bulletin*, 146(11), 941–969.

Elsabbagh, M., & Johnson, M. H. (2016). Autism and the social brain: The first-year puzzle. *Biological Psychiatry*, 80(2), 94–99.

Klin, A., Micheletti, M., Klaiman, C., Shultz, S., Constantino, J. N., & Jones, W. (2020). Affording autism an early brain development re-definition. *Development and Psychopathology*, 32(4), 1175–1189.

Lai, M., Anagnostou, E., Wiznitzer, M., Allison, C., & Baron-cohen, S. (2020). Series Autism 4 evidence-based support for autistic people across the lifespan: Maximising potential, minimising barriers, and optimising the person – environment fit. *The Lancet Neurology*, 4422(2), 1–18.

Lockwood, P. L. (2020). Is there a 'social' brain? Implementations and algorithms. *Trends in Cognitive Sciences*, 24(10), 802–813.

Mercado, E., Chow, K., Church, B. A., & Lopata, C. (2020). Perceptual category learning in autism spectrum disorder: Truth and consequences. *Neuroscience and Biobehavioral Reviews*, 118(January), 689–703.

Palmer, C. J., Lawson, R. P., & Hohwy, J. (2017). Bayesian approaches to autism: Towards volatility, action, and behavior. *Psychological Bulletin*, 143(5), 521–542.

Press, C., Kok, P., & Yon, D. (2020). The perceptual prediction paradox. *Trends in Cognitive Sciences*, 24(1), 13–24.

Rizzolatti, G., & Sinigaglia, C. (2010). The functional role of parieto-frontal mirror circuit: Interpretations and misinterpretations. *Nature Reviews Neuroscience*, 11, 264–274.

Rizzolatti, G., & Sinigaglia, C. (2016). The mirror mechanism: A basic principle of brain function. *Nature Reviews Neuroscience*, 17(12), 757–765.

Robertson, C. E., & Baron-Cohen, S. (2017). Sensory perception in autism. *Nature Reviews Neuroscience*, 18(11), 671–684.

Rosen, N. E., Lord, C., & Volkmar, F. R. (2021). The diagnosis of autism: From Kanner to DSM-III to DSM-5 and beyond. *Journal of Autism and Developmental Disorders*, 51(12), 4253–4270.

Rozenkrantz, L., Mello, A. M. D., & Gabrieli, J. D. E. (2021). Enhanced rationality in autism spectrum disorder. *Trends in Cognitive Sciences*, 25(8), 685–696.

Schaafsma, S. M., Pfaff, D. W., Spunt, R. P., & Adolphs, R. (2014). Deconstructing and reconstructing theory of mind. *Trends in Cognitive Sciences*, 19(2), 65–72.

Stark, E., Stacey, J., Mandy, W., Kringelbach, M. L., & Happé, F. (2021). Autistic cognition: Charting routes to anxiety. *Trends in Cognitive Sciences*, 25(7), 571–581.

Tversky & Kahneman (1974). Judgment under uncertainty: Heuristics and biases. *Science*, 185, 1124–1131.

van de Cruys, S., Evers, K., van der Hallen, R., van Eylen, L., Boets, B., de-Wit, L., & Wagemans, J. (2014). Precise minds in uncertain worlds: Predictive coding in autism. *Psychological Review*, 121(4), 649–675.

Yon, D., Gilbert, S. J., de Lange, F. P., & Press, C. (2018). Action sharpens sensory representations of expected outcomes. *Nature Communications*, 9(1), 1–8.

Chapter 2

Autism Spectrum Disorder

Insights from a Neuroscientific Perspective

Luca Casartelli

Facing the heterogeneity of autism from a clinical and research perspective

There is no doubt that autism awareness has grown significantly in the last two decades. This is particularly evident in high-income countries, but it is also generally true all around the world. Beyond more or less important differences reported in distinct epidemiological studies, autism is widely recognized as a serious concern for individuals with a diagnosis of ASD, for families, for caregivers (e.g., school), for public health systems, and more generally for society (Hyman et al., 2020; Lord et al., 2022). According to the Diagnostic and Statistical Manual of Mental Disorder – version 5 (DSM-5), diagnosis of ASD needs the presence of three symptoms referring to the social domain, and at least two symptoms referring to the repetitive and restricted behaviors/interests domain (APA, 2013). DSM-5-based diagnosis of ASD captures several diagnostic labels that in previous DSM versions were named differently (e.g., Autistic Disorder; Asperger's Syndrome; Pervasive Developmental Disorder-Not Otherwise Specified; Childhood Disintegrative Disorder). Pros and cons of the unique diagnostic label proposed in the DSM-5 have been widely debated in the literature, and arguments supporting (or not) this choice go beyond the general aims of this chapter (for more details, see Rosen et al., 2021). As sketched in Chapter 1, autism is both a medical condition requiring – for example – appropriate differential diagnosis and a form of neurodiversity characterized by a "neurodivergent profile" of strengths and weakness (Lai et al., 2020). As a medical condition, autism encompasses a certain degree of disability that results from

DOI: 10.4324/9781003100140-3

specific – even if largely unknown – neurobiological underpinnings. As a form of neurodiversity, autism can benefit from the characterization of the construct of autistic functioning. Recent debates have sometimes polarized these views as alternative, and mutually exclusive. In contrast, probably we would benefit from considering them together. Indeed, it is self-evident that certain aspects of autism should be clinically treated as medical aspects resulting in disability, whereas others should be treated as "atypical profile of functioning". This point is one of the most challenging and promising issues raised from the last decades of research on autism (Lai et al., 2020). Autism has a "double face", and clinical, rehabilitative, and habilitative management of autism should take into account this "double character". Autism is a neurodevelopmental disorder that changes with and affects development (Lord et al., 2022). The term "heterogeneity" often associated with autism, refers both to the significant inter-individual variability in phenotypical manifestations and intra-individual variability in phenotypical manifestations across the life span. The term "heterogeneity" also refers to differences in etiology, and care needs over time by individuals with ASD. Furthermore, heterogeneity also concerns the presence, number, severity, and nature of co-occurring medical conditions (e.g., epilepsy or gastrointestinal disorders), mental health disorders (e.g., anxiety or attention deficit/hyperactivity disorder – ADHD), and a range of challenging behaviors (e.g., aggressivity or sleep difficulties). Another aspect of heterogeneity in the domain of autism reflects differences in females compared with males. Generally speaking, autism has been considered for decades a "male dominant" condition. Nowadays, multiple reports suggest a higher rate of underdiagnosis, misdiagnosis, and later diagnosis in females compared to males (Harrop et al., 2024). In a UK population-based study, with equal clinical signs of ASD in a group of girls and a group of boys, the diagnosis of ASD was found to be less likely in girls than in boys (Russell et al., 2011). A number of factors can play a role in explaining this result, and in more recent years this study has been re-considered critically. For example, some scholars hypothesized that disparity may reflect sociocultural factors impacting the application of diagnostic criteria, differences in sensitivity in the screening and diagnostic measures (although large-scale studies do not seem to provide support for this hypothesis), and differences in resilience mechanisms or even protective factors. To date, there is no general consensus, and the question about gender differences in autism remains open. Nevertheless, it seems reasonable to claim that underrecognition of autism in females may play a role in explaining differences in prevalence between females and males, and this strongly encourages clinicians in paying specific attention to such a point (Constantino and Charman, 2016). The multiple meanings of the term "heterogeneity" in the context of autism also help to explain why a single assessment or a single session treatment cannot be sufficient. From the one side, autism is a relatively specific condition being defined by the intersection of social and sensory domain peculiarities, restricted and repetitive interests/behaviors. From the other side, autism is *one of many* neurodevelopmental disorders, with which it shares a number of phenotypical manifestations and neurobiological underpinnings. Thus, autism is both a specific condition and a condition with significant overlap with other neurodevelopmental conditions. This raises considerable concerns in the context of early differential diagnosis, considering that in infancy and toddlerhood it can be difficult to clearly disentangle behavioral symptoms related to distinct neurodevelopmental disorders (e.g., ADHD).

A self-evident concern that any scholar faces when the role of neuroscience findings is considered in the context of autism (e.g., genetics, neuroimaging, electrophysiology, etc.) is the distance between the promises of basic research and its real impact for a single individual with ASD. A simplistic analysis may be tempted to claim that neuroscience is scarcely useful for – let us to use imaginary examples – Samir (an 8-year-old child with ASD), Sarah (a 5-year-old child with ASD), Kim (a 16-year-old adolescent with ASD), or Maria (a 35-year-old woman with ASD). This is obviously a simplistic and misleading conclusion, and the crucial role of neuroscience in the context of autism can be easily understood by making a comparison with the recent COVID-19 pandemic events. In the first months of 2020, initial pressing needs were clearly oriented in providing practical support (e.g., promotion of social distancing, supplying protective equipment, and increasing hospitals' capacities). However, the parallel unprecedent efforts in boosting basic research have permitted fundamental steps forward in understanding the virus (e.g., variants, transmission, treatment, etc.). Returning to autism, it is clear that we cannot simply await that basic neuroscience provides a "definitive solution" for autism. Notably and most importantly, probably there does not exist a "definitive solution for autism" in the common sense of the term in medicine (autism cannot be treated as a viral infection, as also recalled in other parts of the book). A reasonable framework should recognize both the (long-term) crucial role of basic research in autism (e.g., to address potential multifactorial causes) and the fundamental need to invest considerable efforts in addressing the current real-life Samir, Sarah, Kim, and Maria's (and their families') needs (Lord et al., 2022).

Interpretation and misinterpretation of biomarkers research in autism

In line with the growing body of studies in neurological and neuropsychiatric domains (e.g., Alzheimer's disease and Parkinson's disease), over the past few decades biomarker discovery has represented one of the key goals of neuroscience also in the context of autism. Generally speaking, the term "biomarker" refers to a quantitative, objectively measured and evaluated characteristic that can provide reliable indication of normal or pathological biological process; biomarker is also used to "map" a pharmacological response to a therapeutic intervention. However, such a generic definition of biomarker risks to be vague, and its operational use misleading. Thus, more recent works tried to deconstruct distinct uses of the term "biomarker", providing a more rigorous and operationally effective categorization. We can distinguish between *diagnostic* biomarker, *stratification* biomarker, *prognostic* biomarker, *predictive* biomarker, and *risk/likelihood* biomarker. A diagnostic biomarker is a measurable characteristic used to detect or confirm the presence of a specific condition or disorder, whereas a stratification biomarker is used to identify more homogeneous biological subgroups within or across a specific categorical label (e.g., individuals with ASD without intellectual disability). A prognostic biomarker identifies the likelihood of a specific clinical event, or recurrence of a specific event, or progression of clinical symptoms in patients with a particular diagnosis. A predictive biomarker identifies individuals who are more likely than comparable individuals without the biomarker to experience a positive or negative effect from exposure to a treatment, clinical intervention, drugs, etc. Finally, the risk/likelihood biomarker indicates the potential for developing a condition or disorder in an individual who does not currently have that condition or disorder (Loth et al., 2021). Considering such a premise on distinct functional meanings of the term "biomarker", an intricate question may concern the state of the art regarding biomarker research in the context of autism. Indeed, although there is a growing body of studies in the field, the focus on the specific meaning of biomarker (i.e., diagnostic, stratification, prognostic, predictive, or risk/likelihood) in the domain of autism is scarce. Nevertheless, the last few decades have testified considerable attention in neurocognitive functions potentially playing a critical role in explaining both pathophysiology and phenotypical manifestations of autism, and they have been often considered in the literature as "putative biomarker of autism". In summary, although it often lacks a clear sub-categorization (e.g., diagnostic, stratification, prognostic, predictive, or risk/likelihood biomarker) that may have helped in operationalizing biomarker research into concrete clinical applications, research findings on autism over the last few decades deserve attention. So, be aware that we strongly support this kind of research, but at the same time we encourage scholars in making more efforts toward building a conceptual and methodological architecture capable of operationally organizing these findings. In other words, we praise researchers' efforts in looking for what has been generally called "putative biomarker of autism", but we also recommend deeper attention in considering operational and functional meaning of the term "biomarker" in daily clinical practice. Thus, for the sake of simplicity and coherence, when we will refer to major neuroscience findings in the context of autism research, we will use the simpler term "marker" to avoid any misleading assumption or misinterpretations. This does not limit the importance of these results, but permits to avoid clinical overinterpretation. In summary, we would like to stress that a putative marker of autism may assume strong clinical relevance, but we do not directly claim that any putative marker of autism is reliable and efficient for supporting diagnosis, as well as stratification, prognosis, and risk or prognosis prediction.

Autistic symptomatology is not always related to autism

Even if – according to the DSM-5 – clinical diagnosis of ASD is based on behavioral symptoms (social domain, restricted and repetitive behaviors/interests), the scientific community strongly agree in considering that not only the study of neurobiological underpinnings but also the study of peculiar neurocognitive functioning and environment is fundamental to understand autism. As anticipated, in the last few decades specific neurocognitive functions (e.g., attention, perception, multisensory integration, etc.) have been each time considered as the cornerstone to understand autism. Using a more prudent attitude, one can claim that atypical developmental trajectories of specific neurocognitive functions should be treated as crucial aspects that – in the context of autism – deserve significant consideration. Neuroconstructivism (Karmiloff-Smith, 2009) and its more recent version (e.g., computational neuroconstructivism; see Astle et al., 2023) are fundamental framework in which neurocognitive functions assume a strong relevance for development. A general idea that largely benefits from classical neuroconstructivism views assumes that innate (or at least very early), low-level, not-detailed, and not domain-specific functions have a crucial role in the development of more complex, high-level, and domain-specific functions. In addition, classical neuroconstructivism views assume that genes, brain, cognition, and environment interact multidirectionally (Karmiloff-Smith, 2009). Thus, a general idea is that (very) early derailments in developmental trajectory of a basic function may have an impact on the development of more complex functions. Let us take a specific neurocognitive function such as multisensory integration as an illustrative example. The ability of processing basic multisensory stimuli – such as a tennis ball (= visual stimulus) and the sound it produces bouncing on the floor (= auditory stimulus) that "refer" to a specific and unique event (i.e., "the tennis ball bouncing on my dining room floor") – is related to the ability of processing more complex multisensory stimuli. Complex multisensory stimuli are, for example, the speech ones (i.e., the sound of the word "*bye*", and the lip movements one needs to produce "*bye*"). A neuroconstructivist framework assumes that early derailments in the developmental trajectories of basic multisensory processing abilities (i.e., tennis ball bouncing on the floor) can have an impact on the development of more complex "social" skills (e.g., language). Thus, neuroconstructivism is a theoretical framework that strongly supports the benefit of investigating basic neurocognitive functioning in autism, being the development of basic neurocognitive abilities potentially related to more complex social skills. This general framework raised considerable enthusiasm in the last few decades (Wallace et al., 2020), although more prudent perspectives are probably desirable (Feldman et al., 2018). Invoking prudence is reasonable for at least two reasons: (1) although theoretically appealing, it is not always so easy to experimentally demonstrate a direct and robust link between basic and more complex neurocognitive functions. Some experimental studies lacked in confirming such a link. This does not mean that the neuroconstructivist framework is meaningless, it probably means that the link between basic and complex functions should be considered in light of multilevel and multivariate relationships between basic and complex functions. Furthermore, (2) clinicians and researchers should be aware – as incisively pointed out by Lord and Bishop (2021) – that "autism spectrum disorder symptoms are not always related to autism spectrum disorder". Thus, atypical attentional processing or atypical sensory processing does not necessarily mean that one individual should have a diagnosis of ASD. Using the social domain as an illustrative example, this message should be clearer. The authors stress the need of considering that statements about social deficits (e.g., an individual does not respond when someone tells him/her something) *can be* – but *not necessarily is* – a sign of autism. This means that they are not specific to autism (i.e., a number of different clinical disorders may entail them), and they are not the primary deficits in autism (even if – for sure – they are important aspects that deserve considerable attention in the context of autism). Furthermore, a simple statement such as "Behavior often disrupts family life" (see the Social Communication Disorders Checklist – SCDC, reported in Lord and Bishop, 2021) may not mean the same thing for parents, family members, caregivers, or individuals with or without ASD. The fact that "autism spectrum disorder symptoms are not always related to autism spectrum disorder" (Lord and Bishop, 2021) can also be tackled from a neuroscientific perspective comparing – for example – behavioral symptoms of cerebellar cognitive affective syndrome (CCAS) and ASD.

The cerebellum is a fascinating brain structure that – in the last decades – has raised considerable interest in the neuroscientific literature. This is mainly due to the fact that the cerebellum was initially considered a purely motor structure (e.g., involved in balance, posture, and motor control), whereas in more recent years its crucial role also in the processing of higher, nonmotor functions has been demonstrated (Leiner et al., 1986; Buckner, 2013; Diedrichsen et al., 2019). Noteworthy, perinatal primary injury to the cerebellum has been hypothesized to have cascade effects on the development of neurocognitive functions whose functioning is normally associated with cortical regions. Such a phenomenon has been defined as "developmental diaschisis" (Wang et al., 2014), and it assumes strong clinical relevance considering that the human cerebellum has also a protracted temporal developmental window (and, in turn, vulnerability window) compared to other cortical brain structures (Wang et al., 2001; Sathyanesan et al., 2019). CCAS is considered an umbrella term that groups a heterogeneous set of symptoms due to distinct pathophysiological mechanisms involving the cerebellum (e.g., malformation, agenesis, acquired lesion, degeneration, etc.). In the literature, this heterogeneous set of symptoms has been also referred to as "dysmetria of thought", and it includes a range of nonmotor symptoms (and – obviously – also motor symptoms). Among nonmotor symptoms, neurocognitive (e.g., attention, perception, sensory processing, language, etc.) and cognitive-affective (e.g., emotional processing, personality changes, etc.) ones have been considered. More recently, also symptoms related to the social domain have been considered in the context of CCAS. Noteworthy for the aims of this book, in the literature clinical manifestations of CCAS have been often referred to as "autistic-like behaviors". If one also considers that in basic neuroscience research cerebellar circuits alterations have been implicated in the pathophysiology of autism (although how exactly this involvement should be considered in clinical terms for individuals with ASD is far to be clarified) (Stoodley, 2016; see also Laidi et al., 2022), and that early injuries to the cerebellum have been considered a significant risk factor for ASD (Wang et al., 2014), one may be tempted to claim that the ASD diagnosis should be strongly related to "something" (e.g., altered anatomy, altered functioning, disrupted functioning, etc.) related to the cerebellum. We suspect that such an assumption is simplistic and misleading, and further critical observations in the context of CCAS should help to clarify such a point. In parallel, such a comparison should help in clarifying more deeply also putative neurobiological underpinnings of autism, and specific features of the autistic functioning. Taken together, an in-depth analysis of the CCAS supports very well the idea that "autism spectrum disorder symptoms – *such as atypical neurocognitive functions or difficulties in social functioning* – are not always related to autism spectrum disorder" (*italic* is ours) (Lord and Bishop, 2021). Let us see it in more detail.

Individuals with ASD and CCAS seem to share a number of symptomatic patterns in a wide range of neurocognitive functions (e.g., biological motion processing, multisensory integration, etc.). Even admitting that this assumption is reliable at the phenotypical level (one may argue that they are only *at first glance* similar, whereas they conceal subtler differences even at the phenotypical level), it is reasonable to hypothesize that the pathophysiological mechanisms leading to these phenotypical profiles are different in ASD and CCAS. For example, one may hypothesize that atypical attentional mechanisms in ASD may derive from failure or derailment in attentional developmental trajectories, whereas in CCAS atypical attentional mechanisms may be primarily due to the loss or reduction of cerebellar inputs to cerebral cortex. These are just illustrative hypotheses, but they should clarify the idea that similar phenotypical manifestations (e.g., atypical attentional profiles) are not necessarily due to the same pathophysiological mechanisms. This observation also reflects the fact that autism is a neurodevelopmental condition (i.e., one can hypothesize that a range of "aspects" are developing in an atypical way), whereas it is hypothesized that CCAS primarily reflects a specific loss/reduction of cerebellar functioning (e.g., in terms of cortico-cerebellar connectivity). Thus, basic and cognitive neuroscience approaches may help in clarifying distinct neurophysiological underpinnings of (at first glance) similar symptoms. In turn, this may promote a deeper analysis of phenotypical manifestations (maybe ascertaining slight differences also at the behavioral level). Behavioral analysis, as it has been referred in the previous chapter, is particularly useful to deconstruct behaviors trying to elucidate the computations (or "reasons") driving them. Comparing ASD and CCAS, it emerges that phenotypical manifestations of autism are primarily driven by atypical "processing rules" (that we have tried to depict with the construct of "autistic functioning"), whereas CCAS is primarily characterized by specific alterations in cerebellar anatomy/functioning that can result in neurocognitive (e.g., attention, perception, sensory processing, and language) and cognitive-affective (e.g., emotional processing, personality changes, etc.) symptoms. This wide range of symptoms just *resemble* to the set of phenotypical manifestations ascribable to the autistic functioning. To characterize what is *primarily ascribable* to autism, and what is *just resemble* to autism, it is crucial to maximize reliability of the diagnosis and efficiency of clinical intervention (Casartelli et al., 2018a). Autism is a complex neurodevelopmental condition that calls individuals with ASD, families, caregivers, clinicians, researchers, and, more generally, society to very demanding challenges. To minimize or even neglect crucial differences (e.g., superimposing conditions that have "just" phenotypical overlap) risks to undermine many efforts.

Candidate neurocognitive marker of autism

We have tried to argue that neuroscientific research in the context of autism can play an important and promising role for future clinical applications, even if we should be aware that simplistic overconfidence in these findings may result in misleading clinical uses. Overconfidence in biomarker research is probably the most evident example. Having clarified our prudent attitude, it is time for providing a brief overview of main neuroscientific findings in the context of autism. For sure, a number of exhaustive and comprehensive reviews of the literature have been published in the last decade, and they should be considered the main reference for clinicians and researchers (among many others, see Casartelli et al., 2016, 2018b; Kessler et al., 2016; Robertson and Baron Cohen, 2017; Zhou et al., 2018; Lai et al., 2020; Courchesne et al., 2020; Constantino et al., 2021; McClellan et al., 2024). A detailed description of recent advancements in the understanding of the neurobiology of ASD – from genetics to brain imaging studies – would probably go beyond the general aims of this book. Technical aspects concerning the role played by genetic factors in explaining – for example – pathophysiology, epidemiology, co-occurring conditions, or heritability of autism are profitably debating in scientific journals (among many others, see Havdahl et al., 2021; Rolland et al., 2023). Similarly, putative brain alterations, for example, focusing on specific brain structures (e.g., Laidi et al., 2022) or in terms of altered brain asymmetry (Postema et al., 2019), and also approaches combining genetics and neuroimaging (e.g., "neurogenetics", see Rasero et al., 2023) have been explored. These lines of "basic" research are surely extremely important, but their understanding can be difficult even for experts in the field. Even more dangerous, a non-specialist reader may easily be confused by *in itinere* conclusions that sometimes articles in scientific journals suggest. In other words, when one reads something like "these findings *indicate* altered brain connectivity patterns in the specific population ABC" in an article published even in a well-established scientific journal, probably he/she should intend "these findings *are consistent with the hypothesis that / can support the hypothesis that* there are altered brain connectivity patterns in the specific population ABC". In addition, he/she would be aware of the caveats of the specific experimental design (e.g., if it is a group-level population analysis, the result cannot be *directly* attributed to any single individual with ABC). To avoid misunderstanding and useless quick recaps of complex neuroscientific findings, here we propose some specific insights for general readers interested in autism (e.g., teachers, caregivers, policymakers, etc.). First of all, we would like to underline to need of prudence for avoiding simplistic or misleading clinical conclusions. In addition, we want to remind that we are just proposing illustrative examples (among many others available) that we suppose can be useful to catch some general insights on the topic.

One hypothesis is that attentional processing can be atypical in autism, and in turn it can be considered a neurocognitive marker of ASD. Attention is a complex, domain-general, and cross-modal (i.e., one can – for example – speak about *visual* attention or *auditory* attention) neurocognitive function. Although in the literature it has often been treated as a monolithic construct, more recent studies underline distinct aspects that can be more profitably treated separately. For example, attentional resources can be allocated following at least three "rules": first, attentional resources can follow a sort of spotlight mechanisms (e.g., from left to right; from up to down). This is a very basic and intuitive characteristic, and anyone can easily refer to the fact that one individual orients attention in different directions. A second rule can refer to the so-called zoom-lens attentional mechanisms. Attention can be modulated similarly to the zoom of a camera: from the one hand, an individual can focus his/her attention on a specific detail (e.g., one specific leaf of the tree), and this can be called "zooming-in" mechanism; from the other hand, an individual can focus his/her attention on the global picture (i.e., the tree), and this can be called "zooming-out" mechanism. The dynamic between seeing the leaf or the tree (and similarly, seeing the tree or the forest) has been considered a crucial way to investigate neurocognitive atypical profiles in autism. Inflexible and hyper-focused attentional profile has been often related to putative difficulties in disengagement of visuo-spatial attentional resources (Corbetta and Shulman, 2002; Ronconi et al., 2013; Keehn et al., 2017). A third feature that seems to characterize the modulation of attentional resources concerns their allocation in space (Carrasco, 2011). Studies in the neurotypical population show that visual attention that requires spatial scrutiny elicits an area of attenuated excitability in the immediate surrounding of the attentional focus. In neurotypical population, this means that there is a specific attentional profile that maximizes the allocation of attentional resources in the center of the attentional focus, limiting the resources in the immediate surrounding of the attentional focus. More simply, it means that neurotypical individuals tend to allocate resources in the center of the attentional focus, limiting the allocation of resources in the immediate proximity of the attentional focus. This architecture of the allocation of the attentional resources should promote both a reliable processing of specific targets (i.e., targets in the attentional focus) and segregation of potential distracting stimuli in proximity of the target. In children with ASD, this dynamic equilibrium has been found to be altered, providing behavioral and electrophysiological (electroencephalography [EEG]-based) evidence that may support the clinically well-established tendency to sensory overload in autism (Ronconi et al., 2018). Here again, we should be clear: this study does not solve or definitively explain why a certain number of individuals with ASD are prone to experience sensory overload. This study can "simply" be considered consistent with such clinical evidence, and it may "simply" provide an argument supporting such a hypothesis. Neuroscience, similarly to any scientific endeavor, needs prudence (and replicability). Scientific arguments are fundamental to support or reject a specific clinical or experimental or theoretical hypothesis, but they should be considered together with other (supporting and contrasting) arguments. Neuroscience needs multiple lines of evidence converging to one specific explanation to reasonably corroborate a hypothesis. Researchers should help general readers in understanding both potentialities and risks of overestimating scientific findings.

A second hypothesis widely explored in the last two decades in the neuroscientific literature concerns potential altered sensory and perceptual processing in individuals with ASD, which in turn – according to a neuroconstructivist framework – may impact the development of more complex (e.g., social) skills. Beyond the interest on specific perceptual functions (e.g., coherent motion processing, biological motion processing, etc.) (for a review and meta-analysis, see Federici et al., 2020), a more general premise deserves consideration. Why should we be interested in considering the way through which individuals with ASD process – for example – the visual scene of two interacting partners? Why should we be interested in understanding how individuals with ASD process – for example – others' face?

The answer is quite simple, but its importance is often underestimated. The way through which one acts and interacts in the world strongly depends on the way through which he/she *sees* the world. For example, if watching a detective movie you are distracted by your smartphone, you may miss some important details concerning the main character's facial expressions; in turn, you may infer misleading conclusions concerning the main character's role in the fraud. How you process visual details (e.g., position of the eyebrow, typical facial expression reflecting genuine worries, etc.) is fundamental to understand the intrigue, and set your attitude towards characters (e.g., I am sympathetic with him or not). Now, we should be clear: not *all* details are relevant, not *all* details are important to disentangle the intrigue of the movie (set aside the fact that you may have a "plan b" such as demanding to your sister who is watching the movie with you). The main strength of neurotypical individuals regards the ability to find a sort of "balance" between processing of important details and neglecting irrelevant ones (to avoid excessive visual overload, putatively resulting in disorientation or confusion or impasse). Atypical patterns of analysis of the visual scene may represent a critical lens to understand potential building blocks of peculiar social functioning in autism. An interesting model proposed in the literature considered distinct levels of processing of the visual scene. This model basically claims that when one naturally looks in a scene, he/she can benefit from at least three levels of analysis: (1) pixel-level (e.g., color, intensity, and orientation), (2) object-level (e.g., size, solidity, and structure of the objects), and (3) semantic-level (e.g., the "meaning" of a man that runs away from a restaurant) (Wang et al., 2015; Robertson and Baron Cohen, 2017). The dynamic equilibrium among these levels results in the effective visual scene mapping. Let us consider an illustrative example. Having reached the mountaintop after a long walk, you may be attracted by enjoying the wonderful view. If you are calm and relaxed, you probably allocate the largest part of your neurocognitive resources to benefit from all details (e.g., contrast of colors between rocks and snow) of the wonderful view (i.e., you would probably focus most of the resources for the so-called "pixel-level"). If you are looking for marmots because that part of the mountain is renowned for their presence, you probably try to disentangle if that "spot" is a small bush or a marmot (i.e., you would probably focus a considerable part of resources for the so-called "object-level"). If you are waiting for your friend, and you glimpse a human figure, you probably allocate most of resources to disentangle if she is calling for help or she is simply saying hello to you (i.e., the so-called "semantic-level"). Neuroscientists try to understand how these mechanisms are regulated benefiting both from refined "behavioral" approaches (e.g., mapping individual visual scene parsing with quantitative eye-tracking methods, and clustering these data through artificial intelligence algorithms; see Wang et al., 2015) and approaches investigating neural underpinnings of these functions (e.g., with electro- or magnetoencephalography approaches, EEG/MEG; with neuroimaging magnetic resonance-based approaches such as functional magnetic resonance imaging, fMRI) (Kessler et al. 2016; Robertson and Baron Cohen, 2017). Although their detailed description goes beyond the general aims of this chapter, recent works have tried to combine the idea that we should look for a "dynamic equilibrium" (i.e., stability and flexibility dynamic) between distinct computations contributing to visual scene mapping, and the state-of-the-art cognitive neuroscience approaches (among many others, see, e.g., Seymour et al., 2019; Ronconi et al., 2020; Knight et al., 2023). A further interesting insight focusing on the dynamic combination of stability and flexibility comes from studies on sensory processing. Thus, let us briefly refer to this aspect.

A third view concerning putative sensory processing anomalies in autism can be useful to understand the critical role of sampling rules in supporting our actions and interactions. A general idea in cognitive neuroscience is that the brain has an architecture that supports multiple parallel and hierarchically organized processing stages, and they have a fundamental role in our understanding of the sensory world. Notably, brain tends to balance *stability* (i.e., when the "external" and "internal" conditions are approximately fixed, it processes according to a coherent and consistent rule), and *flexibility* (i.e., when the contingent physical or contextual conditions change, the brain tries to find a different rule that may result in a "new" stability) (Casartelli, 2019). The case of multisensory integration is illustrative. Among other studies, recently it has been emphasized that multisensory integration is not a monolithic process, whereas it combines distinct low-level and high-level computations (Murray et al. 2016). More simply, in "deciding" whether two stimuli are coming from the same source (e.g., one red flash and one beep-sound coming or not from the alarm system), the brain weighs both low-level features (e.g., the temporal lag between the visual and auditory stimulus) and high-level features (e.g., there is a technician working on the alarm system, and it may happen that he makes some tests). Using cutting-edge EEG-based cognitive neuroscience analyses, it has been suggested that children with ASD and neurotypical children use different "rules" for regulating this dynamic between low-level and high-level features (Ronconi et al., 2023). This does not suggest that individuals with ASD are not able to integrate stimuli coming from distinct sensory modalities, whereas it would "simply" mean that they are benefiting from a "different" rule. A further note is needed: if one limits the argument stating that the rules are "different", one may intend that it is just a different perceptual propensity (as one would say: "I like blue jumper, you like green jumper"). This is only a part of the story. Indeed, it is evident that sometimes (not always, but at least *sometimes*) these "different" sensory/perceptual rules that characterize the autistic functioning have cascade effects that are not functional to daily life activities (e.g., sensory overload). This is a critical and challenging point for further research in the context of autism: should we change the world for creating everywhere autistic-friendly environment, or should we promote clinical intervention that aims to "modify" these different rules? Suppose we have to endorse the first way, are we concretely able to do it? Suppose we have to endorse the second one, are we concretely able to do it? Probably we are far from giving an answer to these points; and even more critically, honestly speaking we are not sure – from an ethical point of view – which of the two ways should be followed. A step-by-step, prudent, and proactive attitude that combines both a pragmatic approach (i.e., we have to address the needs of daily life individuals with ASD) and a "pioneering" approach (i.e., scientific endeavor implies that for promoting progress we have to invest resources also in trying to design "future scenarios") is likely the most reasonable attitude (Lord et al., 2022).

References

American Psychiatric Association (APA). (2013). *Diagnostic and statistical manual of mental disorders, 5th edition (DSM-5)*. Washington (DC), American Psychiatric Publishing, Inc.

Astle, D. E., Johnson, M. H., & Akarca, D. (2023). Toward computational neuroconstructivism: A framework for developmental systems neuroscience. *Trends in Cognitive Sciences*, 27(8), 726–744.

Buckner, R. L. (2013). The cerebellum and cognitive function: 25 years of insight from anatomy and neuroimaging. *Neuron*, 80(3), 807–815.

Carrasco, M. (2011). Visual attention: The past 25 years. *Vision Research*, 51(13), 1484–1525.

Casartelli, L. (2019). Stability and flexibility in multisensory sampling: Insights from perceptual illusions. *Journal of Neurophysiology*, 121(5), 1588–1590.

Casartelli, L., Molteni, M., & Ronconi, L. (2016). So close yet so far: Motor anomalies impacting on social functioning in autism spectrum disorder. *Neuroscience and Biobehavioral Reviews*, 63, 98–105.

Casartelli, L., Riva, M., Villa, L., & Borgatti, R. (2018a). Insights from perceptual, sensory, and motor functioning in autism and cerebellar primary disturbances: Are there reliable markers for these disorders? *Neuroscience and Biobehavioral Reviews*, 95, 263–279.

Casartelli, L., Federici, A., Biffi, E., Molteni, M., & Ronconi, L. (2018b). Are we "motorically" wired to others? High-level motor computations and their role in autism. *The Neuroscientist: A Review Journal Bringing Neurobiology, Neurology and Psychiatry*, 24(6), 568–581.

Constantino, J. N., & Charman, T. (2016). Diagnosis of autism spectrum disorder: Reconciling the syndrome, its diverse origins, and variation in expression. *The Lancet Neurology*, 15(3), 279–291.

Constantino, J. N., Charman, T., & Jones, E. J. H. (2021). Clinical and translational implications of an emerging developmental substructure for autism. *Annual Review of Clinical Psychology*, 17, 365–389.

Corbetta, M., & Shulman, G. L. (2002). Control of goal-directed and stimulus-driven attention in the brain. *Nature Reviews Neuroscience*, 3(3), 201–215.

Courchesne, E., Gazestani, V. H., & Lewis, N. E. (2020). Prenatal origins of ASD: The when, what, and how of ASD development. *Trends in Neurosciences*, 43(5), 326–342.

Diedrichsen, J., King, M., Hernandez-Castillo, C., Sereno, M., & Ivry, R. B. (2019). Universal transform or multiple functionality? Understanding the contribution of the human cerebellum across task domains. *Neuron*, 102(5), 918–928.

Federici, A., Parma, V., Vicovaro, M., Radassao, L., Casartelli, L., & Ronconi, L. (2020). Anomalous perception of biological motion in autism: A conceptual review and meta-analysis. *Scientific Reports*, 10(1), 4576.

Feldman, J. I., Dunham, K., Cassidy, M., Wallace, M. T., Liu, Y., & Woynaroski, T. G. (2018). Audiovisual multisensory integration in individuals with autism spectrum disorder: A systematic review and meta-analysis. *Neuroscience and Biobehavioral Reviews*, 95, 220–234.

Harrop, C., Tomaszewski, B., Putnam, O., Klein, C., Lamarche, E., & Klinger, L. (2024). Are the diagnostic rates of autistic females increasing? An examination of state-wide trends. *Journal of Child Psychology and Psychiatry, and Allied Disciplines*. 10.1111/jcpp.13939

Havdahl, A., Niarchou, M., Starnawska, A., Uddin, M., van der Merwe, C., & Warrier, V. (2021). Genetic contributions to autism spectrum disorder. *Psychological Medicine*, 51(13), 2260–2273.

Hyman, S. L., Levy, S. E., Myers, S. M., & Council on Children with Disabilities, Section on Developmental and Behavioral Pediatrics. (2020). Identification, evaluation, and management of children with autism spectrum disorder. *Pediatrics*, 145(1), e20193447.

Karmiloff-Smith, A. (2009). Nativism versus neuroconstructivism: Rethinking the study of developmental disorders. *Developmental Psychology*, 45(1), 56–63.

Keehn, B., Westerfield, M., Müller, R. A., & Townsend, J. (2017). Autism, attention, and alpha oscillations: An electrophysiological study of attentional capture. *Biological Psychiatry Cognitive Neuroscience and Neuroimaging*, 2(6), 528–536.

Kessler, K., Seymour, R. A., & Rippon, G. (2016). Brain oscillations and connectivity in autism spectrum disorders (ASD): New approaches to methodology, measurement and modelling. *Neuroscience and Biobehavioral Reviews*, 71, 601–620.

Knight, E. J., Freedman, E. G., Myers, E. J., Berruti, A. S., Oakes, L. A., Cao, C. Z., Molholm, S., & Foxe, J. J. (2023). Severely attenuated visual feedback processing in children on the autism spectrum. *The Journal of Neuroscience: The Official Journal of the Society for Neuroscience*, 43(13), 2424–2438.

Lai, M. C., Anagnostou, E., Wiznitzer, M., Allison, C., & Baron-Cohen, S. (2020). Evidence-based support for autistic people across the lifespan: Maximising potential, minimising barriers, and optimising the person-environment fit. *The Lancet Neurology*, 19(5), 434–451.

Laidi, C., Floris, D. L., Tillmann, J., Elandaloussi, Y., Zabihi, M., Charman, T., Wolfers, T., Durston, S., Moessnang, C., Dell'Acqua, F., Ecker, C., Loth, E., Murphy, D., Baron-Cohen, S., Buitelaar, J. K., Marquand, A. F., Beckmann, C. F., Frouin, V., Leboyer, M., Duchesnay, E., ... EU-AIMS LEAP Group. (2022). Cerebellar atypicalities in autism?. *Biological Psychiatry*, 92(8), 674–682.

Leiner, H. C., Leiner, A. L., & Dow, R. S. (1986). Does the cerebellum contribute to mental skills?. *Behavioral Neuroscience*, 100(4), 443–454.

Lord, C., & Bishop, S. L. (2021). Let's be clear that "autism spectrum disorder symptoms" are not always related to autism spectrum disorder. *The American Journal of Psychiatry*, 178(8), 680–682.

Lord, C., Charman, T., Havdahl, A., Carbone, P., Anagnostou, E., Boyd, B., Carr, T., de Vries, P. J., Dissanayake, C., Divan, G., Freitag, C. M., Gotelli, M. M., Kasari, C., Knapp, M., Mundy, P., Plank, A., Scahill, L., Servili, C., Shattuck, P., Simonoff, E., ... McCauley, J. B. (2022). The Lancet Commission on the future of care and clinical research in autism. *Lancet (London, England)*, 399(10321), 271–334.

Loth, E., Ahmad, J., Chatham, C., López, B., Carter, B., Crawley, D., Oakley, B., Hayward, H., Cooke, J., San José Cáceres, A., Bzdok, D., Jones, E., Charman, T., Beckmann, C., Bourgeron, T., Toro, R., Buitelaar, J., Murphy, D., & Dumas, G. (2021). The meaning of significant mean group differences for biomarker discovery. *PLoS Computational Biology*, 17(11), e1009477.

McClellan, J. M., Zoghbi, A. W., Buxbaum, J. D., Cappi, C., Crowley, J. J., Flint, J., Grice, D. E., Gulsuner, S., Iyegbe, C., Jain, S., Kuo, P. H., Lattig, M. C., Passos-Bueno, M. R., Purushottam, M., Stein, D. J., Sunshine, A. B., Susser, E. S., Walsh, C. A., Wootton, O., & King, M. C. (2024). An evolutionary perspective on complex neuropsychiatric disease. *Neuron*, 112(1), 7–24.

Murray, M. M., Lewkowicz, D. J., Amedi, A., & Wallace, M. T. (2016). Multisensory processes: A balancing act across the lifespan. *Trends in Neurosciences*, 39(8), 567–579.

Postema, M. C., van Rooij, D., Anagnostou, E., Arango, C., Auzias, G., Behrmann, M., Filho, G. B., Calderoni, S., Calvo, R., Daly, E., Deruelle, C., Di Martino, A., Dinstein, I., Duran, F. L. S., Durston, S., Ecker, C., Ehrlich, S., Fair, D., Fedor, J., Feng, X., ... Francks, C. (2019). Altered structural brain asymmetry in autism spectrum disorder in a study of 54 datasets. *Nature Communications*, 10(1), 4958.

Rasero, J., Jimenez-Marin, A., Diez, I., Toro, R., Hasan, M. T., & Cortes, J. M. (2023). The neurogenetics of functional connectivity alterations in autism: Insights from subtyping in 657 individuals. *Biological Psychiatry*, 94(10), 804–813.

Robertson, C. E., & Baron-Cohen, S. (2017). Sensory perception in autism. *Nature Reviews Neuroscience*, 18(11), 671–684.

Rolland, T., Cliquet, F., Anney, R. J. L., Moreau, C., Traut, N., Mathieu, A., Huguet, G., Duan, J., Warrier, V., Portalier, S., Dry, L., Leblond, C. S., Douard, E., Amsellem, F., Malesys, S., Maruani, A., Toro, R., Børglum, A. D., Grove, J., Baron-Cohen, S., … Bourgeron, T. (2023). Phenotypic effects of genetic variants associated with autism. *Nature Medicine*, 29(7), 1671–1680.

Ronconi, L., Gori, S., Federici, A., Devita, M., Carna, S., Sali, M. E., Molteni, M., Casartelli, L., & Facoetti, A. (2018). Weak surround suppression of the attentional focus characterizes visual selection in the ventral stream in autism. *NeuroImage Clinical*, 18, 912–922.

Ronconi, L., Gori, S., Ruffino, M., Molteni, M., & Facoetti, A. (2013). Zoom-out attentional impairment in children with autism spectrum disorder. *Cortex; a Journal Devoted to the Study of the Nervous System and Behavior*, 49(4), 1025–1033.

Ronconi, L., Vitale, A., Federici, A., Mazzoni, N., Battaglini, L., Molteni, M., & Casartelli, L. (2023). Neural dynamics driving audio-visual integration in autism. *Cerebral Cortex (New York, N.Y.: 1991)*, 33(3), 543–556.

Ronconi, L., Vitale, A., Federici, A., Pini, E., Molteni, M., & Casartelli, L. (2020). Altered neural oscillations and connectivity in the beta band underlie detail-oriented visual processing in autism. *NeuroImage Clinical*, 28, 102484.

Rosen, N. E., Lord, C., & Volkmar, F. R. (2021). The diagnosis of autism: From Kanner to DSM-III to DSM-5 and beyond. *Journal of Autism and Developmental Disorders*, 51(12), 4253–4270.

Russell, G., Steer, C., & Golding, J. (2011). Social and demographic factors that influence the diagnosis of autistic spectrum disorders. *Social Psychiatry and Psychiatric Epidemiology*, 46(12), 1283–1293.

Sathyanesan, A., Zhou, J., Scafidi, J., Heck, D. H., Sillitoe, R. V., & Gallo, V. (2019). Emerging connections between cerebellar development, behaviour and complex brain disorders. *Nature Reviews Neuroscience*, 20(5), 298–313.

Seymour, R. A., Rippon, G., Gooding-Williams, G., Schoffelen, J. M., & Kessler, K. (2019). Dysregulated oscillatory connectivity in the visual system in autism spectrum disorder. *Brain: A Journal of Neurology*, 142(10), 3294–3305.

Stoodley C. J. (2016). The cerebellum and neurodevelopmental disorders. *Cerebellum (London, England)*, 15(1), 34–37.

Wallace, M. T., Woynaroski, T. G., & Stevenson, R. A. (2020). Multisensory integration as a window into orderly and disrupted cognition and communication. *Annual Review of Psychology*, 71, 193–219.

Wang, V. Y., & Zoghbi, H. Y. (2001). Genetic regulation of cerebellar development. *Nature Reviews Neuroscience*, 2(7), 484–491.

Wang, S. S., Kloth, A. D., & Badura, A. (2014). The cerebellum, sensitive periods, and autism. *Neuron*, 83(3), 518–532.

Wang, S., Jiang, M., Duchesne, X. M., Laugeson, E. A., Kennedy, D. P., Adolphs, R., & Zhao, Q. (2015). Atypical visual saliency in autism spectrum disorder quantified through model-based eye tracking. *Neuron*, 88(3), 604–616.

Zhou, H. Y., Cai, X. L., Weigl, M., Bang, P., Cheung, E. F. C., & Chan, R. C. K. (2018). Multisensory temporal binding window in autism spectrum disorders and schizophrenia spectrum disorders: A systematic review and meta-analysis. *Neuroscience and Biobehavioral Reviews*, 86, 66–76.

Chapter 3

Autism Spectrum Disorder
Communicating Diagnosis

Laura Villa

Communicating diagnosis is a complex process that requires extensive attention, considering that clinicians have to face multiple and multilayered needs. Notably, due to the unavailability of definitive quantitative indexes or biological markers (i.e., there does not exist any laboratory or imaging examination to confirm or exclude the diagnosis), today the diagnosis of ASD is based on the assessment of behavioral manifestations. However, instrumental examinations can be useful for differential diagnosis (e.g., to exclude specific types of encephalopathies). It is important to rely on specialized healthcare centers, and on a multidisciplinary team that includes different but synergetic competences (guidelines suggest the presence of child neuropsychiatrist, psychologist, speech therapist, and neuropsychomotor therapist). The team works closely to provide a global and comprehensive assessment. Gold-standard procedures for the diagnosis of autism provided by a medical doctor entail the use of specific clinical tests, such as the Autism Diagnostic Observation Schedule – 2nd Edition (ADOS-2) and the Autism Diagnostic Interview-Revised (ADI-R). ADOS-2 is a clinical test based on the observation provided by expert clinicians of game sessions; ADI-R is a clinical interview provided by clinicians to parents in order to investigate the presence of specific behavioral manifestations ascribable to autism. During the diagnostic procedure, it is necessary to assess also individuals' cognitive functioning, adaptive skills, language, and potential psychopathological conditions that may co-occur with autism. Clinical interviews with parents are useful to put together information concerning the individuals' behaviors, notably focusing on early phases of development. This is important to have a picture of the developmental

DOI: 10.4324/9781003100140-4

milestones already acquired (or not), especially concerning the psychomotor, linguistic, and social development.

Communicating diagnosis of ASD requires time and considerable prudence. Indeed, a diagnosis of ASD to some extent offers a "label" for referring to specific difficulties shown by toddlers, or children, or adolescents or adults. This label has both the potentiality to promote positive cascade effects and the risk of triggering negative reactions.

The lack of sympathetic involvement in communicating diagnosis risks aggravating – rather that moderating – the burden of the diagnosis, which is *per se* heavy and often goes along feelings of loneliness. Parent(s)[1] often point to an excessively rigid attitude by clinical stakeholders, both at the time of diagnosis and in the following diagnostic steps.

At the level of patient/caregivers *versus* doctor communication and relationship, the role of clinical specialists in autism is surely crucial. Parent(s) are generally more prone to be positive and to recognize the reliability of the diagnostic process when they have the opportunity to make questions, and even to repeat the same questions when it is felt as necessary. Parent(s) appreciate to be rigorously and timely informed, and when they perceive a sympathetic attitude.

Communicating diagnosis to family members

The moment in which the diagnosis of ASD is communicated represents for many families a crucial milestone: sometimes it is perceived as a starting point, at other times it is perceived as an unexpected announcement that hurts and paralyzes. Similarly, communicating diagnosis can represent the final step of a more or less linear, more or less long-lasting, and more or less exhausting diagnostic process; sometimes the diagnostic process is undertaken to find an answer, at other times it hopes to exclude a concern. Parent(s) often deal with the diagnostic process overwhelmed by different – and not rarely discordant – experiences and information.

Diagnosis sometimes represents the final step of a process requested by parent(s), while at other times it has been suggested or even demanded to parent(s) to do it. Parent(s) often cannot neglect suggestions raised by teachers, pediatricians, or relatives; this *de facto* forces parent(s) to undertake a diagnostic screening, but it is not without consequences. Individual propensity to pay attention to clinicians is often biased by the fact that the diagnostic screening is actively requested or passively undergone.

Nevertheless, the diagnostic screening is always a complex process that requires rigorous information, clear explanations, and sympathetic support, considering that the diagnosis of ASD grounded exclusively on behavioral manifestations.

Clinically and scientifically rigorous information is crucial considering that, nowadays, ASD is considered a spectrum disorder; DSM-5 recognizes multiple phenotypical profiles for ASD well beyond the outdated stereotypic view that considered ASD mainly related to intellectual disability. When intellectual disability or other clear signs of developmental delays are present (e.g., severe language or severe motor delay), parent(s) are normally aware that something is not covering the typical developmental trajectory. In contrast, in cases in which there is not any clear delay but there are subtle, blurred, and fluctuating troubles (e.g., socio-communicative, concerning the pattern of interests, etc.), parent(s)' understanding of the scenario can be more difficult. This is particularly demanding considering that these subtle, blurred, and fluctuating phenotypical manifestations are age-dependent (i.e., atypical behaviors are not identical across development) and can be mixed with effects related to potential co-occurred neurodevelopmental conditions (e.g., attention deficit and hyperactivity disorder [ADHD], language disorder, etc.). In addition, a further potential variable that should be taken into account concerns the fact that atypical patterns of behaviors can be attributed to "simple" individuals' temperament or character; it is more likely that it happens in cases in which there is not intellectual disability or clear signs of developmental delay, and when similar (maybe more attenuate) behavioral attitudes can be found in the broader familiar context (e.g., uncle, grandfather, etc.).

Another important variable in determining parent(s)' reactions is the way in which the diagnosis is communicated. Clarity and gradualness seem to be key elements: parent(s) who receive a large amount of information seem to be generally more satisfied than those who judged the amount of information received as merely adequate. Some parent(s) want to receive as much information as possible, even if they do not fully understand it; in contrast, other parent(s) prefer to receive a minimal amount of information, and leave to clinical services the responsibility of setting rehabilitative programs.

Sometimes, parent(s)' propensity to look for multiple consultations can result in an excessive charge that may overwhelm them. Generally, parent(s) that take several consultations by distinct clinical experts experience more negatively the communication of the diagnosis than parent(s) that undergo a more linear (and quick) diagnostic process. This is not surprising, considering that the burden of uncertainty during the diagnostic process is significant, and enlarging this period beyond the necessary time for having rigorous diagnosis is not desirable.

To explain and to support are also critical aspects when clinicians communicate a diagnosis of ASD; indeed, it is crucial to provide parent(s) with clear insights on the atypical (and age-dependent) functioning that characterizes individuals with ASD. Rigorous and punctual behavioral analysis during clinical assessment should support clinicians in providing examples of atypical functioning that can be clearly understood by parent(s). Notably, behavioral manifestations of atypical functioning are core elements supporting the clinical diagnosis, combined with standardized best practice procedures (e.g., ADOS-2). When clinicians and parent(s) share their views on a specific and well-characterized behavior observed during clinical assessment (e.g., during a standardized test or during a session of shared interaction), a sort of syntonization can be promoted. Reconsider a specific episode, sequences of a specific game, or specific parts of a clinical test may contribute to promote a shared view of the observed atypical behaviors, bypassing the simplistic (but necessary) communication of a diagnostic label that cannot fully describe the multilayered complexity of autism.

To illustrate the peculiar manifestations of the atypical functioning results in a shared and dynamic approach that promotes a potential paradigm shift in managing atypical behaviors, and reasonably fosters a better outcome.

To limit the communication of the diagnosis to a simplistic categorical "label" it would be misleading for parent(s), and it may potentially have negative cascade effects in the promotion of positive and proactive attitude.

Clinicians observe a multitude of reactions when a diagnosis of ASD is communicated, and often these reactions do not correlate with the patients' clinical picture or contextual scenario. Indeed, these reactions are also strongly modulated by parent(s)' personal attitude and character. Parent(s) can experience anger, sense of guilt, and even embarrassment, and not necessarily they are mutually exclusive feelings. Parent(s) can promote protective mechanisms that minimize, rationalize, deny, or even amplify the burden of the diagnosis and the spectrum of difficulties described by the clinician. Parent(s) may desire, or even be sure, that rapid and efficient intervention can definitively solve any problem.

Any disability raises considerable concerns in parent(s), notably considering the future and the impossibility to have a clear picture of potentialities, difficulties, and reasonable outcomes. Parent(s) are forced to think about the future without having the means and tools to prefigure it. Parent(s) wonder about their child's future daily life, and there are no clear answers because the questions are *per se* very complex, multilayered, and challenging. In addition, some questions seem to be premature: "Will he/she learn to read? How much his/her life will be conditioned by this diagnosis? Will he/she be able to have an independent life, or a romantic relationship?". Other questions are self-directed, and they concern parent(s)' future possibility to work, travel, or go to a concert again.

In addition, learning that autism is a lifelong condition often amplifies the distress experienced by parent(s), raising concerns about the future, and the potential need of taking care of him/her continuously, and the serious troubles raised by the possibility that he/she may be left alone after the parent(s) are passed away.

Often the scale of events throws parent(s) into a state of despair, and the experience is often comparable to a sort of emotional paralysis; parent(s) often feel misunderstood, powerless, unsure of the choices to be made. A frequent reaction in response to the diagnosis is to try to find the "cause" of the disorder, or to ask for more tests, or to contact different clinical specialists. It may also happen that the limited understanding of the neurobiological underpinnings of the disorder – basically due to the fact that generally parent(s) are not expert clinicians or researchers (e.g., they are not geneticists or neuroscientists) – can result in a feeling of being to some extent responsible for the diagnosis; in turn, this results in strong feelings of guilt and self-incrimination among parent(s).

Even when the feeling of guilt is not present, parent(s) may blame themselves for not having realized the problem earlier, or for not having sought help in a persistent way ("If someone had told me clearly what it was, then I would not have wasted at least three or four years waiting for who knows what").

A common state of mind experienced after guilt is anger. This is a generalized feeling that leads parent(s) to wonder why this happened to them, what they did wrong. Parent(s) often feel offended when dealing with parents who take their children's health for granted.

Although it is an extremely serious situation, notification of the diagnosis is not always exclusively negative. Some parent(s) report that they were relieved when they were able to contact specialists.

Thus, the communication of a diagnosis of ASD can also go with positive feelings. It can help to give a specific denomination to a series of difficulties that probably seemed heterogeneous and fluctuant; it can help to overtake the impasse due to the lack of a label, and the uncertainty concerning the potential strategy to carry out. To receive a label – even if anguishing – can serve as a starting point to orient future choices, the research of clinical service, educational support, and rehabilitative treatment.

Accordingly, the diagnosis can help to trigger positive and proactive reactions that can boost new balances within family members, with new roles and new tasks. Parent(s) can also feel a sort of relief when they find into the specific diagnostic label a putative explanation for the relational difficulties experienced with their child. Parent(s) experienced considerable difficulties in promoting an effective emotional synchronization with their child, and often this results in questioning their parenting style. Nowadays, the scientific community is concordant in claiming that autism does not concern the parental style, but autism has specific – even if largely unknown – neurobiological underpinnings.

Feelings of self-confidence about the efficacy of the parental support can play a positive role promoting new chances, interventions, and finally can help to limit the stress related to the burden of the diagnosis. In contrast, low level of confidence in the efficacy of parental support may result in a tendency to delegate (to other familiar members, to the school, to the clinical service, etc.) the key decisions of the rehabilitative challenge.

Parent(s)' attitude is also influenced by the efficacy of the relationships within and outside the nuclear family.

A robust network of well-disposed people supporting parent(s) in the period in which the diagnosis is communicated assumes a crucial role in modulating stressful reactions, notably considering that the diagnosis of ASD likely represents one of the most challenges to tackle in the future.

However, in situations of persistent parental stress, which is common in parent(s) of individuals with ASD, there is less perception of social support, so it may happen that parent(s) are not fully aware of the resources and possibilities that their network could provide.

Coping strategies are an additional important factor in modulating parental stress. Coping is defined as the cognitive and behavioral effort to deal with specific demands (internal and external) that are assessed as excessive and exceeding an individual's resources. Classically, three main coping strategies are identified in the literature: problem-oriented coping strategy, emotion-centered coping strategy, and avoidance-oriented coping strategy. To be prone mainly to the problem-oriented coping strategy has been associated with stress reduction and better quality of life, although the multifaceted scenario of human experience requires prudence in claiming simplistic conclusions.

Communicating diagnosis outside the nuclear family

Comeback after the diagnostic process resulting in a diagnosis of ASD is an additional important milestone. Parent(s) face expectations, desires, or even denials experienced by relatives or close friends that have not participated directly in the diagnostic process; notably, relatives or close friends probably are not well prepared about the features of the autistic functioning or potential steps that need to be done. The significant set of information received by parent(s) from clinicians is – in this moment – a crucial support to reply to genuine feelings expressed by relatives and close friends. The presence of overlapping co-diagnosis (e.g., ADHD and language disorder) and in turn the blurred, multifaceted, and complex phenotypical manifestations of ASD worsen the difficulties experienced by parent(s) in explaining the scenario.

Here again, the presence of clearly atypical developmental trajectories (e.g., intellectual disability, marked learning difficulties, etc.) makes relatives' and close friends' recognition of the diagnostic label easier. Often, parent(s) start from the most evident and easily understandable phenotypical trait to share the result of the diagnostic process. In contrast, in case in which phenotypical troubles are subtle, blurred, and fluctuating (e.g., in the socio-communicative domain, concerning the pattern of interests, etc.), to communicate the diagnosis of ASD to relatives and close friends is even more complicated. Indeed, they are more often considered as temporary troubles that can be overtaken simply across time, and in turn they do not need any specific and major intervention. An additional aspect that deserves to be considered concerns the potential presence of the so-called "broader autism phenotype". One of the parents or close relative (e.g., grandfather or uncle) may present subclinical traits ascribable to the core of the autistic functioning (e.g., more or less soft difficulties in the social domain, more or less marked behavioral routines or very circumscribed range of interests, etc.). The presence of an individual in the broader familiar context with such peculiarities sometimes represents an important proactive aspect that promotes and supports the understanding of the diagnosis. Other times it happens the opposite: the presence of similar phenotypical manifestations in a member of the familiar context may result in a sort of denial of the diagnosis, and this amount of peculiar phenotypical manifestation is simply considered one of the numerous variations of individual character.

Parent(s) often express the desire not to communicate immediately the diagnosis, as if this would somehow constitute protection *for*, but also *by*, grandparents, relatives and close friends, and notably for younger members of the nuclear family (e.g., sisters and brothers). This may in some cases be a reasonable and understandable choice to limit additional strain.

Communication of the diagnosis can – on the one hand – represent the final statement around a dismissed hope (i.e., "then it is really true, there is a problem") and – the other hand – can provide the trigger to dramatically declare the end of a doubt about parent(s)' educational responsibility; this finally supports the attribution of undeniable (although largely unknown) neurobiological and genetic counterparts to autism, clarifying once for all that those behavioral troubles are not related to any educational or parental misconduct.

Having said that, communicating the diagnosis to the broader nuclear family remains a delicate step: a child on whom doubts, uncertainties, and hopes have been placed, who has often been taken for clinical and diagnostic examination without the unanimous consent (sometimes parents do not agree on this choice), returns home with a specific diagnostic label. This label seems to erase all previous relationships as if it were impossible to maintain the bond that existed with the child before the starting of the diagnostic process. However, returning home accompanied by specific hints concerning the autistic functioning can support the mobilization of promising resources.

Comeback home supported by hints from clinicians such as "it can be done in this way" can mobilize new and more effective resources even in the broader nuclear family.

The communication of the diagnosis is the watershed not only for parent(s) and the nuclear family, but more generally for the broader familiar context: it raises different positions when faced with such an event, it shows and reveals doubts and fears and – in some ways – repositions more or less functional previous balances.

The familiar network in some cases represents the real safety net. The possibility of activating not only new resources but also specific skills and roles that can be assumed by distinct members of the network assumes a pivotal strategic importance. Not all members of the family system necessarily have to take up new positions, but the division of tasks according to specific skills and abilities can in several situations be a solution that allows the numerous new challenges to be carried out with less effort.

Sometimes parent(s) adopt a "wait-and-see" attitude: "Tell it when the time is right". Often this position hides the hope that a medical error during the diagnostic process has occurred, and that excessive emphasis has been placed on the interpretation of certain atypical behaviors, or that there is a general and widely exaggerated tendency toward over-medicalization. Similarly, there is the idea that perhaps the individual that has received the diagnosis of ASD, mostly in cases in which the diagnosis is very early, will change rapidly. In other words, it may happen that parent(s) try to deny the categorial stability that the diagnosis of ASD entails (as it will be clarified later, the diagnosis of ASD entails age- and context-dependent phenotypical manifestations, but the stability of the diagnostic label across time is widely recognized in the literature, with important exceptions as it will be explained in Chapter 5). Parent(s) may hypothesize that the diagnosis was hasty, also considering that – as already stated – to date there is not a single quantitative biomarker able to support *individual* diagnosis (although the last few decades have shown a huge progress in clarifying the neurobiological architecture of ASD, and more generally the role of biomarkers at the group level in aggregate analysis). In other words, parent(s) may hope that heterogeneous behavioral manifestations, phenotypical fluctuations related to the changes in the contextual scenario, and more generally the peculiar developmental trajectories that characterize autism may reflect an additional factor supporting an alleged diagnostic mistake.

At first glance, a diagnosis of ASD can be characterized by opposite aspects: from one side, the nosography label is stable although changes in behavioral manifestations related to development and contextual scenario persist. From the other side, the literature reports a certain percentage of cases in which individuals lose diagnosis. If it is possible – and eventually how – scholars can keep together these seemingly opposite tendencies which will be discussed in the next chapters.

Communicating diagnosis to siblings

The presence of older or younger siblings poses an immediate challenge related not only to the possibility of communicating the diagnosis per se, but maybe primarily *when* and potentially even more challenging *how* to communicate it.

Parent(s) often have spent considerable amount of time in specialized clinics, and coming back at home is often combined with the burden of the diagnostic process resulting in the diagnosis of ASD.

From one side, the nature of the brotherly relationship may evolve more positively following a clear explanation of the "sources" of those atypical (and sometimes hard-to-understand) behaviors.

However, there are several variables that should be taken into account as they may reverse the situation. Age, personal attitudes, character, sociodemographic context, and sometimes previous questions (e.g., "Why does he/she react in this manner? Why does not he/she talk? Why does not he/she play with me?) are components that should be carefully considered.

To communicate the diagnosis may trigger new familiar dynamics that potentially impact the balance among family members. We cannot generalize simplistic conclusions. One cannot say that such a communication will impact positively (or negatively) in any cases. Clinicians should be supportive, and they are called to provide rigorous counseling according to the specificity of the situation.

In early childhood and during primary school, children are naturally inclined to offer help and protection to their siblings that manifest a range of difficulties. In this period they are often unaware of the diagnosis of their sibling, while in adolescence an additional challenge arises for them. They not only have to deal with the classical changes that typically characterize adolescence (e.g., the desire to rebel, the natural desire to break away from the family unit, etc.), but having achieved a (more or less) complete awareness of their sibling's diagnosis, they also need to realize the meaning and implications of that diagnosis for their own lives.

Adolescents with a sibling with a diagnosis of ASD often have to deal with strong emotions. Sometimes these emotions may include certain nuances of negative feelings toward his/her sibling, or the desire to run away from familiar commitments of care, or the desire to share their feelings with peers, or even the fear of losing the attention of parents. Anger and more generally any negative feelings are often followed by a sort of sense of guilt, and various (often reasonable) concerns for the future. If peers taunt the sibling with ASD or do not show an understanding for his/her difficulties, the neurotypical sibling may experience feelings of isolation, shame, and estrangement from the peer group. Conversely, neurotypical adolescents who experience a positive social fabric may face their challenges related to their sibling's diagnosis with proactive and generally positive attitude. This can represent a strong positive factor also for the nuclear family and the broader familiar context.

General suggestions to communicate the diagnosis to neurotypical siblings concern the need to explain it in an open, honest, and developmentally appropriate way. Parent(s) may need to deal with their own thoughts and feelings before they are able to effectively share this delicate information with neurotypical siblings. They can manifest withdrawal or inappropriate behaviors. Clinicians should give in advance notice to parent(s) concerning the need of communicating the diagnosis to neurotypical siblings. It may happen that neurotypical siblings are reluctant to ask about their brothers/sisters being disoriented or confused, and they may be worried about the possibility of hurting parent(s). Even if the complexity and the heterogeneous set of scenarios prevent clinicians from giving a unique, monolithic, and identical for everybody prescription, there is consensus among clinical stakeholders about the need of providing appropriate and update information to neurotypical siblings concerning their brother's or sister's diagnosis. Indeed, disorientation can frequently be a cascade effect of lack of information. When information about a sibling's condition is absent, younger neurotypical children may be worried about the possibility to develop or catch the same "stuff" that leads their sibling to behave in this peculiar and potentially maladaptive way, or they may be even worried to have caused this "stuff". Younger children mainly focus on a couple of atypical behaviors (e.g., their sibling with ASD does not talk, or he/she likes too much to line up his/her toys, etc.), and the recognition of their sibling's condition basically passes for these peculiarities. School-aged neurotypical siblings may wonder to know if their brother or sister with ASD will get worse, and what will happen to them. Adolescents may manifest anxiety and genuine worries about their future responsibility and the future impact their sibling with ASD would have on the family. Parent(s) should be aware that their neurotypical sons/daughters may also experience difficulties and distress. To gain time for them is important, and there are many different ways to spend positive and *exclusive* time with them (e.g., a specific sport activity once a week/month/year; a specific shopping afternoon for their birthday; a specific concert, or theatre, or any other specific opportunity that can represent a unique moment for them, etc.). If parent(s) follow specific clinical programs to foster the interaction with their sons/daughters with ASD, neurotypical siblings can learn a large number of skills from their parent(s) in order to promote a more effective interplay with their siblings with ASD. It is important to underline the fact that neurotypical siblings also need support in this specific and difficult aim. To guarantee neurotypical siblings time, to be patient with them, and to genuinely praise them for their efforts are crucial aspects that need to emphasized. In the best scenario, neurotypical siblings learn to be part of the positive, proactive, and enriching environment together with their parent(s), teachers, relatives, and obviously clinicians. It happens often that neurotypical siblings take on their own responsibilities with respect to their brother/sister with ASD.

For example, sometimes siblings with ASD can be destructive and hard to redirect. They can also be quick to push, bite, or engage in other challenging behaviors with their neurotypical siblings as putative target. Neurotypical siblings must be taught on how to manage these situations. Generally, this should include asking parent(s) for help in handling the situation. Parent(s) should make any effort to allow neurotypical siblings a safer space that could promote and support their development, and at the same time could protect them from the potential aggressive behaviors of their siblings with ASD when no easy solution is available (e.g., when neurotypical siblings are younger).

Neurotypical siblings should be supported in understanding and accepting their feelings, even when they fluctuate between positive and negative feelings. Parent(s) are surely crucial for managing these fluctuations, but a clinical specialist can also be beneficial to tackle such a situation.

Neurotypical siblings need opportunities to experience recreational and playful activities similar to the ones they can observe in peers' families where there is not a diagnosis of ASD. Noteworthy, this need should be considered for the entire nuclear family. Thus, care services supporting families with community programs or special activities may represent a fundamental support for neurotypical siblings and their parent(s).

Neurotypical siblings need opportunities to feel that they are not alone, and that other people can understand and can share – at least partially – certain experiences. Some neurotypical siblings can benefit from attending a "sibling support group" or a "sibling event" where they can talk about their feelings and feel accepted by others who share a common understanding, while also having opportunities for fun without any (more or less conscious) sense of guilt.

Finally, an additional important aspect concerns the fact that parent(s) should help in preparing neurotypical siblings for possible reactions from acquaintances raised by the meeting with their brothers or sisters with ASD.

Communicating a second diagnosis of ASD within the same nuclear family

Communicating the diagnosis of ASD to families who already have a sibling with the same diagnosis is particularly challenging.

This additional charge can significantly impact the hopes and familiar resources not only in economic terms, but also in terms of motivation and forces. It happens that the brother/sister shows a very different clinical picture, and this makes the fact that they are associated with the same diagnosis difficult to be understood. For example, they may have different degrees of developmental delays, different language abilities, and different range of interests that may raise doubts on the reliability of the diagnostic processes.

To date, the literature is consistent in underlining the role of genetics to describe both the co-occurrence of other diagnoses of neurodevelopmental conditions (e.g., ADHD), and the co-occurrence of two or more diagnoses of ASD in the same family. Beyond the focus on complex neurobiological aspects that do not regard this chapter, here a special attention to potential distinct scenarios may be useful.

For example, a second diagnosis of ASD in the same nuclear family may concern the oldest brother (diagnosis that apparently was not made earlier), or the diagnosis to the second-born.

An additional aspect that deserves to be considered concerns the diagnosis in females compared to males. For example, females tend to receive a diagnosis later than males, even if it is complex to identify *which* specific elements (and most importantly *why*) lead to such a delay. Adaptive behaviors, camouflage, or social stereotypes may play a role. Beyond such a point, it is clear that a second diagnosis of ASD in the older sister may be particularly critical to be accepted. To summarize, and despite the fact that differences may occur according to the specific clinical profile (e.g., neurocognitive level, presence or absence of co-occurring conditions, etc.), a growing body of studies ascertain that siblings of individuals with ASD are at higher genetic risk of autism and/or neurodevelopmental disorders than typically developing individuals without siblings with a diagnosis of ASD.

A second diagnosis of ASD in the same nuclear family forces a re-modulation of familiar balances already impacted by the first diagnosis. Here again, familiar style, support from the broader social context (e.g., relative, close friends, school, etc.), and coping strategies play an important role in such a re-modulation. Adaptive resources trying to promote positive synergy with the context are directed to find new balances.

It happens that a sibling who raises lower concerns to the family (e.g., he/she has a better socio-communicative level; he/she has a good cognitive functioning, etc.) is misleadingly considered by the family as the reference for neurotypical development. To undermine this belief with a second diagnosis leads to planting doubts about their capability to recognizing future communicative signals, and more generally his/her functioning.

However, it also happens that the second diagnosis is not unexpected; indeed, many families with a child with ASD participate in specific programs for (very) early surveillance, screening, and eventually detection and diagnosis of ASD in younger siblings.

Although the scientific and clinical importance of such programs is well established, from the viewpoint of families they may be recognized in different ways. For example, for certain families participating in these programs is perceived as a stressful period that characterizes the wait for a final verdict (instead of being considered a useful process assuring a careful evaluation and the timely indication of the presence/absence of potential risk factors). In contrast, certain families are primarily reassured by the fact that these programs will be able to detect any potential signs of anomalies, and in turn – even in the unwanted case of clear signs of autism – an early detection and diagnosis will be guaranteed (with all the positive cascade effects of timely educational and rehabilitative interventions).

Even in the best scenario in which families experience proactively the surveillance programs, the communication of the second diagnosis of ASD entails a significant level of individual, parental, and familiar stress, and we cannot underestimate also potential economic worries. To reorganize the familiar balance may request (more or less) radical changes that may even lead one of the parents to leave his/her previous employment (with potential effect on the family's economic balance).

As sketched before, the presence of supportive broader familiar context may – in these cases – be crucial.

Communicating the diagnosis to him or her

Communicating the diagnosis to the child/adolescent with ASD is something that a family has to face sooner or later; it is possible that a child with good cognitive functioning may ask this question independently, making reference either to his/her own difficulties or to hints provided in different contexts (e.g., schools, media, etc.).

Indeed, there is no "right age" or "right time" in which to explain to a child/adolescent about his/her diagnosis. Individual personality, abilities, and social awareness are all factors to consider in determining when one is ready for receiving communication, information, and explanation concerning his/her diagnosis.

If older when communicated, he/she may be extremely sensitive to any comments more or less directly inferring that he/she is "different". It is important to look for the presence of certain signs that reasonably indicate that he/she could be "ready" (although "ready" probably is not the right word), and they can provide support for taking the decision to communicate him/her such a crucial information. Some children with ASD can actually ask, "What is wrong with me?" "Why cannot I be like everybody else?", or even "What is wrong with everyone?". These kinds of questions can be a potential indication that they need information about their diagnosis. Some children, however, may have similar thoughts, but they are not able to express them so clearly. It even happens that individuals do not get a formal diagnosis until they are in their teens or at an older age. Frequently, those who are diagnosed later have had some negative experiences that can influence the decision concerning the time in which the information about the diagnosis of ASD was shared with them. On the other hand, an older child may – for example – already be aware about other previous diagnoses (e.g., ADHD, conduct disorder, or language disorder); in this case, communicating the co-diagnosis of ASD could be very difficult, although useful.

Many adults with ASD express the opinion that children should receive some information before they hear it from someone else, or overhear or glimpse information that they feel may concern themselves. A child can believe that people do not like him/her or that parent(s) seem to be often troubled without knowing exactly the reason.

Many parents are worried that associating their child with the label "ASD" will make him/her feel wrong, or that he/she may use this label as an excuse to give up and lower the efforts. Adults on the spectrum have often found the opposite to be true. Indeed, to provide information on the peculiarity of his/her differences will result in a better understanding of the complex and multilayered dynamics regulating human behavior, and will foster motivation to support multiple challenges.

One child or adolescent with ASD may know that he/she has a certain number of peculiarities but – like many individuals at certain developmental stages – he/she may come to the wrong conclusion about his/her perceived differences. It happens that children and adolescents with ASD visit doctors and therapists and go for treatments without exactly knowing "why". Even individuals with ASD who do not overtly express any concerns may nevertheless have troubles, doubts, and hesitations about their peculiarities.

Most children and adolescents normally need minimal information to start. More detailed information can be added over time. It is important to explain in simple words the peculiar functioning that characterizes individuals with ASD. This is reassuring because if one parent has understood (or a clinician has understood) his/her peculiar functioning, it means that there is no terrible mystery to explain.

A clinician's support with the specific role of supporting and discussing information about autism, and how it may affect an individual's life over time, can make easier for family members to be seen by the child/adolescent as supportive. A clinical specialist who discusses information with the child/adolescent about his/her condition can also help parent(s) in understanding his/her reaction.

To explain a diagnosis of ASD cannot be realized in one or two sessions: both children and adolescents with ASD normally need time to assimilate new information. It may take weeks or even months before the child/adolescent initiates to make spontaneous comments or to ask further details concerning his/her diagnosis. Once the process of explaining the diagnosis of ASD is started, to make information meaningful for him/her will greatly promote learning processes concerning strategies that can be adopted to manage their own difficulties.

Note

1 For the sake of simplicity, here and hereafter we use the term "parent(s)" to refer – more generally – to the principal caregiver(s). We obviously recognize that the term "parent(s)" does not cover all the spectrum of situations. Be aware that the use of the term "parent(s)" is simply due to the need of focusing on clinical aspects, and it does not conceal any other implicit meanings. We adopted the term "parent(s)" simply because it is appropriate for most cases.

Bibliography

Brogan, C. A., & Knussen, C. (2003). The disclosure of a diagnosis of an autistic spectrum disorder: Determinants of satisfaction in a sample of

Scottish parents. *Autism: The International Journal of Research and Practice*, 7(1), 31–46.

Carlsson, E., Miniscalco, C., Kadesjö, B., & Laakso, K. (2016). Negotiating knowledge: Parents' experience of the neuropsychiatric diagnostic process for children with autism. *International Journal of Language & Communication Disorders*, 51(3), 328–338.

Davis, N. O., & Carter, A. S. (2008). Parenting stress in mothers and fathers of toddlers with autism spectrum disorders: Associations with child characteristics. *Journal of Autism and Developmental Disorders*, 38(7), 1278–1291.

Ekas, N. V., Lickenbrock, D. M., & Whitman, T. L. (2010). Optimism, social support, and well-being in mothers of children with autism spectrum disorder. *Journal of Autism and Developmental Disorders*, 40(10), 1274–1284.

Estes, A., Munson, J., Dawson, G., Koehler, E., Zhou, X. H., & Abbott, R. (2009). Parenting stress and psychological functioning among mothers of preschool children with autism and developmental delay. *Autism*, 13(4), 375–387.

Goin-Kochel, R. P., Mackintosh, V. H., & Myers, B. J. (2006). How many doctors does it take to make an autism spectrum diagnosis?. *Autism: The International Journal of Research and Practice*, 10(5), 439–451.

Hansen, S. N., Schendel, D. E., Francis, R. W., Windham, G. C., Bresnahan, M., Levine, S. Z., Reichenberg, A., Gissler, M., Kodesh, A., Bai, D., Yip, B. H. K., Leonard, H., Sandin, S., Buxbaum, J. D., Hultman, C., Sourander, A., Glasson, E. J., Wong, K., Öberg, R., & Parner, E. T. (2019). Recurrence risk of autism in siblings and cousins: A multinational, population-based study. *Journal of the American Academy of Child and Adolescent Psychiatry*, 58(9), 866–875.

Karst, J. S., & Van Hecke, A. V. (2012). Parent and family impact of autism spectrum disorders: A review and proposed model for intervention evaluation. *Clinical Child and Family Psychology Review*, 15(3), 247–277.

Khanna, R., Madhavan, S. S., Smith, M. J., Patrick, J. H., Tworek, C., & Becker-Cottrill, B. (2011). Assessment of health-related quality of life among primary caregivers of children with autism spectrum disorders. *Journal of Autism and Developmental Disorders*, 41(9), 1214–1227.

Lai, M. C., Anagnostou, E., Wiznitzer, M., Allison, C., & Baron-Cohen, S. (2020). Evidence-based support for autistic people across the lifespan: Maximising potential, minimising barriers, and optimising the person-environment fit. *The Lancet. Neurology*, 19(5), 434–451.

Lyons, A. M., Leon, S. C., Roecker Phelps, C. E., & Dunleavy, A. M. (2010). The impact of child symptom severity on stress among parents of children with ASD: The moderating role of coping styles. *Journal of Child and Family Studies*, 19, 516–524.

Moh, T.A., and Magiati, I. (2012). Factors associated with parental stress and satisfaction during the process of diagnosis of children with autism spectrum disorder. *Research in Autism Spectrum Disorders*, 6(1), 293–303.

Osborne, L. A., & Reed, P. (2008). Parents' perceptions of communication with professionals during the diagnosis of autism. *Autism: The International Journal of Research and Practice*, 12(3), 309–324.

Poslawsky, I. E., Naber, F. B., Van Daalen, E., & Van Engeland, H. (2014). Parental reaction to early diagnosis of their children's autism spectrum disorder: An exploratory study. *Child Psychiatry and Human Development*, 45(3), 294–305.

Rodrigue, J. R., Geffken, G. R., & Morgan, S. B. (1993). Perceived competence and behavioral adjustment of siblings of children with autism. *Journal of Autism and Developmental Disorders*, 23(4), 665–674.

Siklos, S., & Kerns, K. A. (2007). Assessing the diagnostic experiences of a small sample of parents of children with autism spectrum disorders. *Research in Developmental Disabilities*, 28(1), 9–22.

Smith, L. E., Seltzer, M. M., Tager-Flusberg, H., Greenberg, J. S., & Carter, A. S. (2008). A comparative analysis of well-being and coping among mothers of toddlers and mothers of adolescents with ASD. *Journal of Autism and Developmental Disorders*, 38(5), 876–889.

Chapter 4

Autism Spectrum Disorder
Clinical Intervention and Treatment

Laura Villa

Any child with autism spectrum disorder (ASD) has different needs, so the treatment plan needs to be individualized. There is no one-size-fits-all treatment, so the goal of each treatment is to maximize children's abilities in different functions by reducing autistic symptoms and supporting development and learning.

To date, the rehabilitative and habilitative interventions validated by empirical experiences and the literature refer to cognitive-behavioral approaches. According to this perspective, autism is understood as a behavioral disorder with specific neurobiological basis, whose specific elements give rise to a range of behaviors characterized by deficits, excesses, or atypicalities. These behaviors can be modified through specific programs structured in relation to the environment, the individuals, and their needs.

Therefore, cognitive-behavioral approaches promote adaptive behaviors and reduce problematic ones in individuals with ASD through intensive and structured interventions that can be used not only by therapists and clinicians in general, but also by parents.

Alongside the development of behavioral approaches, other models of educational treatment are also emerged. These types of treatments are referred to as "developmental" because they emphasize the importance of following the sequence of typical development in teaching new skills, but they share many similarities with behavioral treatments.

How to choose the "right" intervention?

In general, intervention is highly individualized, and it depends on the assessment of distinct aspects considered during the diagnostic process. To characterize an individual profile is extremely useful in making the intervention as effective as possible, considering that each individual is characterized by specific cognitive, emotional, and behavioral difficulties as well as specific individual strengths. Intervention is typically structured on distinct modules, and it is (or it should be) regularly monitored and revised. For this reason, following a diagnosis of ASD, it is necessary to evaluate the choice of treatment (that may include different intervention methods) with an experienced clinician, possibly involving additional specialized experts in the process.

Considering high inter-individual variability and heterogeneity of symptoms, it is not possible to identify a unique intervention strategy that may fit for all children with ASD. The therapeutic approach must evolve and adapt to the specific individual developmental trajectories. It should also involve a series of interventions aimed at enriching social interaction, increasing communication, and facilitating the enlargement and diversification of interests that in turn may promote more flexible behavioral patterns. Such an approach should be pursued involving both family and the broader contextual environment.

Beyond distinctions among different approaches, it seems to be clear that three core features should characterize any treatment that aims to be effective: (1) it should promote *early intervention*, considering that timing is crucial to foster intervention when the brain is extremely plastic (i.e., the brain structures have not reached full functional specialization; neurocognitive functions are maturing); (2) it should promote *intensive intervention* that can provide a variety of structured situations in which children may diversify and expand their experiences, activities, and models of relationship; and (3) it should promote a *curriculum-based intervention* to structure a sequential order that may support the organization of the therapeutic process, clear definition of objectives, and ongoing monitoring of progress.

In the literature, we can find multiple classifications for interventions; the main classifications are proposed to categorize them following specific criteria, features, or methodologies. Notably, there are interventions grounded on the basics of applied behavior analysis (i.e., Early Intensive Behavioral Intervention and Lovaas Model of Applied Behavioral Analysis), naturalistic developmental behavioral interventions (i.e., Early Start

Denver Model, Incidental Teaching, Enhanced Milieu Teaching, and Pivotal Response Training), developmental interventions (e.g., Developmental Individual Difference Relationship-Based Floortime and Relationship Developmental Intervention), educational interventions (e.g., TEACCH, Family Implemented TEACCH for Toddlers), interventions focused on singular specific behavior grounded on the basics of the applied behavior analysis (e.g., models for interventions using Discrete Trial Training, or Positive Behavior Support, Antecedent-Based Interventions, Extinction Functional Behavior Assessment, Modeling, Prompting, Reinforcement and Differential Reinforcement, and Task Analysis), interventions that focus on naturalistic developmental behavioral approaches (e.g., Joint Attention Symbolic Play Engagement and Regulation), interventions that aim to improve communication and social interaction (e.g., Picture Exchange Communication System, communication interventions involving speech-generating devices, Sign Language Training, Verbal Behavior Therapy, Social Stories, Theory of Mind Training, Comic Strip Conversations, Social Skills Groups Interventions with computers and other technology), intervention mediated by parents (e.g., Psychoeducational Parent Support, Preschool Autism Communication Trial, Parent Education and Counselling, Parent Education and Behavior Management, and Parent Intervention), and psychological interventions (e.g., Cognitive Behavior Therapy).

These interventions reflect intensive and long-term programs based on manual procedures; normally they last more than one year, they require considerable time per week (several hours), and they pursue aims in distinct domains such as communication, social skills, and behavioral adaptation. Focused interventions are basically structured by practices and procedures that can be considered the core constitutive features of comprehensive interventions, although their target is more specific and intensity is generally lower.

Considering that autism can entail medical comorbidities, in addition to these rehabilitative models other interventions can be necessary (e.g., referring to general internal medicine, pharmacology, and pediatrics).

Here, even if the detailed description of every validated approach goes beyond the aims of this book, the main models of intervention and some considerations concerning pharmacological and nutritional interventions will be provided.

Behavioral interventions

Early Intensive Behavioral Intervention (EIBI)

EIBI represents an important comprehensive model of intervention, considering that it focuses on distinct domains (e.g., cognitive functioning, language, sensorimotor abilities, and adaptive functioning) through their long-term development. EIBI is generally proposed from the age of 2/3 years old, which is close to the time of diagnosis (when diagnosis is timely).

During early phases of development, the brain is still extremely plastic (i.e., "adaptable"). The brain plasticity maximizes the possibility to have effective results in the long-term period. Thus, early intervention is crucial because it not only provides the most promising beginning, but also provides more chances for positive prognosis.

EIBI provides individualized, behavioral instructions; it requires a significant time commitment, and it is structured with one-to-one or small-group practices.

Early intervention programs often include family and teacher trainings.

The origin of this approach can be traced back to Skinner's behavioral analysis. According to Skinner, behaviors are developed and/or conditioned by reinforcing consequences. This is referred to as operant conditioning, and the construct of "operant" refers to any behavior that has an impact on the environment, and in turn entails consequences. Each behavior is influenced by what happens after an event through positive or negative reinforcement.

Operant behaviors (actions under individual control) differ from respondent behaviors. Skinner described respondent behaviors as automatic or reflexes (e.g., pull back the hand when one touches a boiling cup).

Skinner's perspective on operant conditioning significantly influenced developmental theories, suggesting that a child's behavior can be modified through positive and negative reinforcement.

Behavioral approaches focus on changing behaviors, and try to clarify what happens before and after the behavior. They are largely accepted among educators and healthcare professionals, and employed in schools and clinical settings. This encourages desired behaviors and discourages undesired behaviors, which in turn promotes the improvement of a variety of skills. Progress is tracked and measured. Applied Behavior Analysis (ABA) involves the systemic teaching of small, measurable units of behavior. Tasks to be learned, based on the individual's developmental profile, choices, and preferences, are broken down into small steps. Each step is taught through repeated and closely spaced teaching sessions, initially in a 1:1 ratio, using specific instructions or discriminative stimuli.

A child is guided to provide simple responses that are systematically incorporated into age-appropriate response repertoires. The learning process architecture is structured to be errorless, using prompts and consequences that effectively serve as reinforcement.

In neurotypical development, an error is often an opportunity to learn. In contrast, children with ASD do not learn making mistakes; when they make a mistake, they seem to learn also the error. For this reason, it is crucial to prevent the possibility that a child with ASD – during a learning process – may also learn an "incidental" error, and to prevent it a specific external guidance is necessary.

The fundamental goal of ABA is to apply the principles of operant conditioning to understand the relationship between the target behaviors and the external conditions, and to implement a series of interventions aimed at the modifying behavior and/or the environment.

The treatment reinforces positive behaviors (such as socialization and language use), discourages negative behaviors (problem behaviors), and identifies target problems that are particularly relevant when they involve potential positive cascade effects also on other individual behaviors.

ABA teaching procedures involve creating a structured environment and using systematic teaching techniques to create a learning environment.

Behavioral analysis is based on the ABC model (A=antecedent; B=behavior; and C=consequence). The "antecedent" refers to the contextual scenario before the target behavior, that is, the specific scenario from which the target behavior is elicited. The "behavior" (or target behavior) refers to any action that can be executed or simply observed. The "consequence" describes what happens after the behavior: it can support or restrain the behavior, it can promote or limit the rate of its occurrence (all things being equal in terms of exposure to the stimulus) according to the more or less reinforcing feedback received directly by the guide or more generally by the environment.

A desired behavior should be reinforced frequently: initially, it may be necessary to reinforce the behavior every time it occurs, but once it is established (i.e., it reliably and consistently occurs) it can typically be maintained using an intermittent reinforcement schedule.

The main learning strategies employed by ABA are the following: *prompting*, *shaping*, *modeling*, *chaining*, *fading*, and *task analysis*. A brief description of each term is provided here.

[**Prompting**]. Prompting is an additional assistance used to guide the response. Prompting is used to support performance and increase the likelihood of a specific behavior occurring. The assistance methods include, in decreasing order of intrusiveness:

- *Physical assistance* (i.e., physically guiding the hand to perform the task)
- *Gestural assistance* (i.e., pointing to the correct response as a visual cue)
- *Model of completed task* (i.e., providing a model or example of the completed task)
- *Verbal assistance* (i.e., providing verbal prompts or cues to perform the task)
- *Demonstration of task execution* (i.e., showing how to perform the task)

- *Visual assistance* (i.e., using visual aids or images to explain how to perform the task)
- *Written assistance* (i.e., providing written instructions on how to perform the task)
- *Intrinsic motivation* (i.e., the task itself is highly motivating for the child)

Providing assistance allows the child to obtain more reinforcement, reducing frustration and increasing motivation.

Error-free learning is guaranteed by applying specific teaching methods as follows:

[Modeling, Shaping]: It involves reinforcing successive approximations to a desired behavioral goal until the goal is achieved. To apply shaping, a behavior that is realistically within the child's capabilities and somewhat similar to the target behavior is selected. That behavior is differentially reinforced until it occurs with a certain frequency. Once a high frequency of the behavior is established, the reinforcement criterion is slightly changed to obtain another behavior that represents a closer approximation to the target behavior. This process continues in successive steps until the desired behavior is achieved.

[Chaining (Forward and Backward)]: Forward chaining involves breaking down a complex task into a sequence of steps and teaching the first step first, then the second, the third, and so on. Backward chaining, on the other hand, involves breaking down a complex task into a sequence of steps and teaching the last step first, then the second-to-last step, and so on.

[Fading]: Since assistance has the disadvantage of inducing dependence, it should be gradually attenuated, moving from more intrusive to less intrusive, as soon as possible. The attenuation of a prompt or unnatural assistance allows the child to respond to more natural stimuli.

[Task Analysis]: It facilitates and motivates learning by making it more predictable and logical, promoting consistency in teaching among different teachers, and assessing teaching and its outcomes for the child. When used as part of a behavior

management program, task analysis is particularly useful in planning for potentially problematic situations such as transitions or unstructured activities.

In the ABA framework, three learning procedures can be considered: Discrete Trial Teaching (DTT), Natural Environment Teaching (NET), and Incidental Teaching.

DDT is a structured approach, whereas NET is a naturalistic approach. NET is grounded on the child's individual motivations, and it concerns situations that can be found in his/her daily life. DDT is generally employed in well-structured environments, and it is commonly referred to as "table task".

DDT is useful to learn some competencies that require the repetition of the specific skill and at the same time are not naturally engaging for children (e.g., imitation, denomination, and receptive skills). NET is especially suitable because it follows the child's specific interests, and it benefits from them establishing specific aims in contextual scenarios that he/she deals with in his/her daily life. DDT focuses mainly on the consequences of the learning steps, whereas NET focuses mainly on the antecedents. Furthermore, DDT entails a specific and structured generalization phase after the learning process, whereas NET entails generalization during the flow of the learning process.

Thus, it is noteworthy to state that DDT and NET are not mutually exclusive nor are they opposed approaches. Classically, NET looks less structured than DDT. Notably, NET requires the therapist to be very aware of the targets that a child has in his/her repertoire and to follow his/her hints as a guide to what will be motivating and engaging for him/her. A common misconception states that if the child is not at the table, then he/she is engaged in a NET. However, this is not always the case. Only when the therapist is benefiting from the child's specific tools and interests in the natural environment that we can speak about NET.

Finally, the Incidental Teaching entails the structuring of the environment in such a way that the child is motivated to engage in the desired target behavior. For example, this can be done by placing attractive objects visible but out of full reach, making only small or incomplete portions of objects to prompt the child to request more. An additional example can be the planning of activities that require the child to seek assistance, such as sabotaging the activity to prompt the child to ask for missing materials. Another example is the introduction of a disruptive element to distract the child from the task or interrupt the activity, in turn prompting the child to point out his/her disappointment. The environmental structuring aims to motivate the child to acquire competences.

Naturalistic developmental behavioral intervention

Considering that naturalistic behavioral treatments adopt strategies that essentially focus on guiding children to learn in their natural environment, they can be considered an evolution of DDT teaching approaches.

Naturalistic behavioral treatments share the principles of ABA with DDT approach. These approaches require teaching behavior procedures in the environment where the behavior naturally occurs, and the use of natural antecedents and consequences (reinforcements) necessary to maintain and promote behaviors.

To consider children's initiative increases their motivation to learn, and in turn it reduces the need for external reinforcements.

Early Start Denver Model (ESDM)

ESDM is an intervention program designed for preschool-aged children with ASD, and developed by Sally Rogers and colleagues in the context of the Developmental Disabilities programs at the University of Colorado Health Sciences Center.

ESDM provides comprehensive support for preschool-aged children with ASD, and it involves the collaboration with parents. It benefits from a series of behaviorally- and developmentally oriented strategies within a relationship-based framework, and this leads to create an emotionally positive environment.

ESDM intervention can be provided at home or in other settings (e.g., school, educational center, etc.) both by trained specialists and parents during natural play and daily routines. ESDM aims to increase the rates of development in every domain and to decrease the symptoms that limit the acquisition of new abilities.

ESDM focuses on the development of communication and reciprocal social interaction skills, and these areas are largely considered core difficulties for individuals with ASD. This intervention program aims to build foundational skills in those areas and then expand its effects to other developmental domains.

ESDM considers autism as a primarily social disorder, and it emphasizes the need for improving social interaction skills in all activities and contexts. It teaches imitation, emotional communication, language, and social play. Communication is a key objective of the intervention, as it is essential for social and familial functioning, academic learning, and the development of functional skills for adulthood.

ESDM incorporates distinct aspects of ABA treatments: it includes systematic data collection and integrates elements of DDT (e.g., individualized sessions with the child and structured teaching procedures). It also incorporates aspects of naturalistic behavioral approaches, placing more emphasis on the child's guide in learning. The 1:1 teaching environment and structured educational setting aim to facilitate rapid learning; notably, they make available materials and play routines from daily life, and they allow the child to choose the learning activities, fostering motivation, social learning, and generalization of skills.

The clinical choice of balancing environmental structuring (from DDT) and child-directed activities (from naturalistic behavioral approaches) largely depends on the abilities that have to be improved, and on the individual developmental trajectory. This complex balance should be attentively evaluated, and eventually distinct directions should be undertaken if they are supposed to be more effective. Teaching sessions carried out at home or at school help in generalizing the acquired skills from the therapeutic setting. The significant parental involvement throughout the intervention is a crucial added value of the entire approach. Parents generally spend a significant amount of time with their child, and they generally know him/her better than anyone else (also considering that children with ASD may have limited participation in or connection with family life).

Parental experience and their involvement as part of the therapeutic "team" promote the generalization of learning to other contexts, and the child's integration into daily life family environment. Parental involvement in the intervention process requires strong motivation, as well as significant commitment in terms of time (e.g., participation in sessions, mutual exchanges with therapists, coordination, etc.).

Similarly, also therapeutic programs carried out at school promote generalization. Mutual collaboration between familiar caregivers and the school is crucial, and it needs periodic consultations and meetings.

Teaching activities proposed in ESDM programs benefit from daily life materials, and it involves daily practices. Object-mediated activities may have cognitive, imitative, and motor objectives, providing opportunities for communication and engagement in dual or small-group interactions to foster the acquisition of social skills.

Pivotal Response Treatment (PRT)

PRT was developed by Robert L. Koegel and Lynn Kern Koegel while working at the Stanford University. It was previously called Natural Language Paradigm. This approach has been used since the 1970s.

PRT is an established intervention for autism derived from ABA, and is based on Naturalistic Developmental Behavioral Intervention principles.

PRT targets pivotal areas of child development, including motivation and social imitation, which in turn promotes more widespread and generalized progress. PRT focuses on embedding learning opportunities throughout daily routines for promoting pleasant and effective learning.

Goals of this approach include the development of communication and language skills, the increase of positive social behaviors, and relief from disruptive self-stimulatory behaviors.

This approach is play-based and is promoted by the child.

The PRT therapist targets pivotal areas of individual development instead of working on one specific behavior. By focusing on pivotal areas (motivation, response to multiple cues, self-management, and imitation of social interactions) PRT produces improvements across other areas of social skills, communication, behavior, and learning, emphasizing natural reinforcement.

The key aspect of PRT is motivational engagement. Therapists take advantage of multiple strategies to identify elements that are meaningful and motivating for each child (e.g., specific objects, activities, or interests) and then use them as reinforcements to promote active participation and learning. PRT is grounded on social learning theory, which supports the notion that intrinsic motivation and interest in an activity are crucial for effective learning.

PRT intervention can be customized based on the specific needs of children.

During therapeutic sessions, the therapist benefits from specific strategies consistent with ABA fundamentals to facilitate the child's interaction and learning. For example, they can use prompting (that involves assisting the child in performing a specific action or responding to a request) or choice incorporation (that allows the child to make choices and have a certain degree of control during therapeutic activities).

An important aspect of PRT is the generalization of learned skills to the child's daily life. Therapists work closely with parents and teachers to promote the application of PRT strategies in different contexts (e.g., home, school, and social situations). This helps children to generalize the learned skills and use them more independently and spontaneously.

Parents can serve as "co-therapists", working in collaboration with the therapist to implement strategies and provide consistent support to the child.

It is important to note that PRT intervention does not replace other therapeutic or educational approaches but can be integrated with forms of intervention to create a comprehensive and personalized treatment plan for each individual child with ASD.

The choice of intervention is based on the specific individual profile, which is crucial for the rigorous assessment provided by clinicians specialized in autism. PRT can be combined with behavioral therapies, language therapies, occupational therapies, and other therapeutic approaches to provide a comprehensive and integrated support for children with ASD.

A key advantage of PRT is that it can be adapted according to age and developmental level. By adjusting strategies and activities, it can be proposed to preschool and school-aged children and adolescents.

It is important to emphasize that PRT intervention also requires specific training for therapists and close collaboration among professionals, parents, and teachers. The involvement and cooperation of all caregivers are crucial to ensure proper implementation of the intervention.

Intervention based on naturalistic developmental behavioral approaches

Joint Attention, Symbolic Play, Engagement, and Regulation (JASPER) model

The JASPER model is an evidence-based intervention grounded on a combination of developmental and behavioral principles developed by Connie Kasari at the University of California, Los Angeles. JASPER is a targeted, modular intervention in the domain of social communication, and it is included in the broader category of naturalistic developmental behavioral interventions. It targets the foundations of social communication (e.g., joint attention, engagement, and play) and uses naturalistic strategies to increase the quality and complexity of social communication.

JASPER model stresses the need of understanding the role of joint attention and symbolic play skills in promoting progress in language, social skills, and cognitive abilities in children with ASD. It focuses on the development of interactive and social communication skills by means of structured and targeted activities.

The primary goal of the JASPER model is the promotion of interaction and mutual communication between the child and the therapist, encouraging active participation and the child's motivation.

Specific objectives can include increasing joint attention activities, encouraging symbolic and imaginative play, promoting imitative behaviors, and regulating emotions.

During therapy sessions, therapists use specific strategies to encourage the child's engagement. These may include the use of interactive toys and materials, modeling appropriate social behaviors, positive reinforcement, and incorporating the child's choices and interests. The goal is to create a stimulation and rewarding environment that could facilitate learning and the development of social and communicative skills.

Interventions based on the JASPER model often actively involve parents in therapy sessions. Parents learn strategies used by therapists and apply them in daily life familiar activities, promoting a conducive environment for the development of their child with ASD, notably for the development of his/her social and communicative skills. Also in this approach parental involvement is essential for the generalization of skills learned during therapy and for promoting their use in real-world contexts.

The JASPER model can lead to significant improvement in joint attention, symbolic play, social interaction, and language skills in children with ASD. It is advisable to work with professionals specialized in autism to evaluate the suitability of the JASPER model for a specific individual with ASD and to develop a personalized treatment plan.

Educational interventions

Treatment and Education of Autistic and related Communication-handicapped Children (TEACCH) program

The TEACCH approach is a model of intervention based on structured education for individuals with ASD. It was developed in the 1970s at the University of North Carolina and has become one of the leading educational approaches in the field of autism.

Founded by Shopler, it is the largest and most influential program dedicated to the treatment of ASD by a state agency.

The main goal of the TEACCH approach is to promote independence, autonomy, and success in learning for individuals with ASD. The approach consists in creating a structured and organized environment that provides clarity, predictability, and support for individuals with ASD.

The main feature that characterizes the TEACCH program compared to most other ones is its comprehensive multidisciplinary nature, and it implies the interaction among services, professionals, and families.

The achievement of independence and social inclusion in adulthood, through structured teaching and the enhancement of individual strengths, is the target of the intervention.

The TEACCH approach is based on several key components:

- *[Visual structure]:* The environment is organized in a visually clear and understandable way, using visual materials such as cards, pictograms, and schedules to provide instructions, give directions, and aid in understanding activities.
- *[Individual work systems]:* Individual work systems are used to guide the child through activities, breaking them down into smaller, manageable steps. This helps the child understand the order of activities and work independently.
- *[Individualized programs]:* Individualized learning programs are developed according to the specific needs and abilities of the child with ASD. These programs focus on specific goals, breaking skills down into successive and progressively more complex steps.
- *[Promoting independence]:* The TEACCH approach aims to support the child's independence by teaching him/her self-management skills (e.g., organizing materials, managing time, and planning activities).
- *[Collaboration with family and scholastic environment]:* The TEACCH approach promotes collaboration with family and scholastic caregivers to ensure the continuity of the approach, and structured environment both at home and at school.

The TEACCH approach is based on a thorough assessment of individual specific abilities, strengths, and challenges. According to this assessment, individualized programs are developed.

The TEACCH intervention lacks objective studies on its effectiveness, considering that most of the renowned studies have been conducted by the same researchers who developed and implemented the program (rather than independent researchers), and they rely primarily on data assessing satisfaction from families and practitioners.

However, since it incorporates many specific elements from other widely tested and objectively validated treatments (e.g.,

DTT, naturalistic behavioral strategies, the use of visual materials, and parent training), the TEACCH intervention is generally considered an effective approach.

It is important to emphasize that the TEACCH approach is not a specific therapeutic approach, but an educational approach that can be integrated with other forms of intervention and can be effective in improving communication skills, socialization, adaptation, and autonomy in individuals with ASD. The structured organization of the environment, the use of visual materials, and the identification of specific goals have been demonstrated to both facilitate progress in learning process and achieve educational objectives.

A distinctive aspect of the TEACCH approach is its flexibility and adaptability to distinct needs and ages. TEACCH interventions can be customized to address specific individual difficulties or behavioral challenges. This supports the implementation of a highly individualized intervention plan that takes into account an individual child's abilities, interests, and needs.

Furthermore, the TEACCH approach promotes active involvement of the family in the educational process. Parents are supported in learning TEACCH strategies and encouraged to use them at home, creating a consistent and supportive environment for the child.

It is important to note that the TEACCH approach is not without criticism and debates in the field of autism. Some scholars argue that the approach may overly emphasize structure and routine, limiting the child's flexibility and independence (that in contrast should be significantly promoted in children with ASD). Therefore, it is crucial that TEACCH interventions are tailored to the individual needs and integrated with other therapeutic and educational approaches.

In conclusion, the TEACCH approach is a model of intervention based on structured education that aims to promote autonomy and learning in individuals with ASD. Through the visual organization of the environment, identification of specific goals, and collaboration with the family, efforts are made to foster the development of social, communicative, and adaptive skills in children with ASD.

Interventions targeting specific skills

These interventions utilize Picture Exchange Communication System (PECS) for language, Social Skill Training for social skills, and training in living skills and autonomy for personal autonomy. The recipients of these interventions are children, adolescents, and adults with specific support needs in certain areas.

Speech language therapy and verbal skills therapy for autism

This type of treatment can help people with ASD to improve their abilities in communicating and interacting with others. This type of intervention can help some individuals to improve their spoken or verbal skills (e.g., correctly naming people and things, better explaining feelings and emotions, using words and sentences better, improving prosody, and nonverbal communication). The three main interventions we refer to are the PECS, Sign Language, and Verbal Behavior.

Picture Exchange Communication System

PECS is a communication system based on the use of pictures to help individuals with ASD in developing functional communication skills. It is a structured and visual method that allows individuals with ASD to communicate their needs, desires, and thoughts using symbolic images. PECS was developed in the 1980s by Andy Bondy and Lori Frost, and it has been widely adopted as a communication tool for individuals with ASD. It is based on the principle that communication is a fundamental right of everyone, and all individuals – regardless of their verbal abilities – can learn to communicate effectively. The PECS teaching protocol is based on Skinner's work "Verbal Behavior", and it applies a broad spectrum of principles from ABA. It employs specific teaching strategies and reinforcement with the aim of promoting increased independence and systematic error correction procedures (that should facilitate learning even in case of errors). Conversely, it does not involve the use of verbal prompts because it aims to immediately promote initiative and avoid dependence on prompts. The PECS system consists of a series of progressively more complex phases:

- *[Phase 1] Picture Exchange:* In this phase, the child learns to exchange a single picture with a communication partner to obtain what he/she wants (e.g., he/she can change a picture of a cookie to receive a cookie).
- *[Phase 2] Distance:* In this phase, the child learns to move away from the communication partner to deliver the picture. This encourages the development of mobility and awareness of social context.
- *[Phase 3] Picture Discrimination:* In this phase, the child learns to discriminate between different pictures and select the correct one to communicate his/her desire or need.
- *[Phase 4] Picture Sequencing:* In this phase, the child learns to combine different pictures to form a more complex communication sequence (e.g., he/she can use a sequence of pictures to request "I want the red cookie").
- *[Phase 5] Spontaneous Labeling:* In this phase, the child learns to label objects, actions, or concepts without the use of pictures. This promotes the development of vocal language.

PECS has been widely used and studied by the scientific community. Many studies have shown that PECS can improve communication skills and social interaction in individuals with ASD. The use of visual images facilitates the understanding and expression of communicative intentions, reducing frustration and increasing the effectiveness of communication.

PECS has many advantages, such as no special training requirement (images are easy to understand and often labeled). It is facilitated by simple matching, and negative emotional experiences associated with language can be avoided by beginning with PECS. Moreover, many individuals with ASD begin with the ability to indicate what they want, so there is a high chance of success. Finally, PECS is a low-tech and relatively inexpensive language intervention. It is important to emphasize that PECS may not be suitable for all individuals with ASD. Some individuals may benefit from other methods of augmentative and alternative communication (e.g., assistive technology or Sign Language). In conclusion, PECS is a picture-based communication system that has proven to be effective in improving the communication skills of individuals with ASD. This approach provides a structured and visual method that facilitates communication and reduces frustration in individuals with limited verbal language abilities. PECS must be used in various contexts, such as home, school, or therapy settings. It can be tailored to the individual needs, allowing for gradual progression along the distinct phases of the system. In addition, PECS can be combined with other therapeutic and educational approaches (e.g., ABA and TEACCH) to provide comprehensive and integrated support.

It is important to emphasize that PECS does not replace the learning of verbal language. In contrast, it represents an initial step in developing functional communication skills, and it can serve as a stepping stone for subsequent verbal language learning. The implementation of PECS requires proper training and support from qualified professionals. Parents and educators can be actively involved in the learning process and encouraged to use PECS in daily routines to ensure consistent and ongoing practice. Due to the use of symbolic images, it offers a structured and visual method that promotes the expression of communicative intentions and social interaction. The ultimate goal of this method is to provide individuals with ASD the necessary tools to communicate most effectively as possible, and to participate as fully as possible in daily life activities.

Sign Language

Sign Language can be particularly useful for individuals with ASD who have difficulties with verbal communication. It can offer an alternative way to express themselves and interact with others. Among others, the relevance and effectiveness of Sign Language in autism are relied on the fact that it is based on visual and gestural cues (rather than verbal language). Individuals with ASD often show greater sensitivity to visual cues than verbal information, making Sign Language a more accessible tool for them. In addition, Sign Language can be more easily understood by individuals with difficulties in comprehending verbal language, and it allows them to get involved in social dynamics more effectively.

Since Sign Language utilizes gestural and visual signs, it can be more easily interpreted by individuals with ASD who may have difficulties in understanding verbal signals, facial expressions, or nonverbal communicative intentions.

The use of Sign Language in autism can also have other significant advantages. One of them is that Sign Language can facilitate mutual understanding between individuals with ASD and neurotypical individuals.

Furthermore, Sign Language can help to promote social interaction and foster the inclusion of individuals with ASD. When their peers, family members, or school professionals learn Sign Language, they can communicate with individuals with ASD more effectively, thereby increasing opportunities for interaction and active participation. This can contribute to support social inclusion and improve the quality of relationships.

It is important to emphasize that the use of Sign Language in autism depends on individual needs and preferences. While some individuals with ASD may significantly benefit from learning and using Sign Language as their primary form of communication, others may prefer alternative and augmentative communication tools (e.g., pictures or assisted communication devices). It is crucial to adopt an individualized approach and respect the choices and preferences of each individual.

The implementation of Sign Language in autism requires adequate training and support from qualified professionals (e.g., occupational therapists and speech language therapists specialized in autism). These professionals can provide specific guidance on learning Sign Language, teaching strategies, and the most effective way to integrate it into the individual's daily context.

Considering these PECS and Sign Language descriptions, which approach should be sponsored?

The choice between PECS and Sign Language in the context of autism largely depends on the individual needs and capabilities. Both systems offer alternative and augmentative communication tools that can be effective in promoting communication and social interaction.

Sign Language is based on the use of gestural and visual signs to represent words, phrases, and concepts. It can be learned through training and practice and requires good hand coordination and the ability not only to understand but also to reproduce the signs correctly. Sign Language can be used for both language comprehension and expression.

On the other hand, PECS is a system of exchanging pictures where individuals with ASD use images or symbols to communicate their desires, needs, and thoughts. PECS is based on the idea that pictures represent a universal language and provides a structured method for teaching communication via the exchange of images. PECS requires the ability to take pictures and exchange them with a communication partner.

The choice between Sign Language and PECS depends on various factors, such as the individual skills and preferences, level of comprehension, motor and cognitive abilities, and the environment in which communication takes place. Some individuals with ASD may benefit from both systems, using them in a complementary manner depending on the context and communication needs.

It is important to work with qualified professionals (e.g., occupational therapists and speech-language therapists specialized in autism) to assess each individual's communication abilities and to determine which communication system is most suitable for their specific needs. In some cases, a mixed approach – combining elements of Sign Language and PECS – may be appropriate to maximize communication and promote the development of language and social skills.

Verbal Behavior

In 1957, Skinner introduced the concept of "verbal behavior" in his work titled "Verbal Behavior". He understood language not only as a form of verbal behavior, but primarily as a learned behavior that is influenced by the same environmental variables and principles governing other behaviors.

Skinner essentially extended the principles of operant conditioning to verbal behavior. He considered language as a behavior that can be studied in relation to the environmental stimuli that precede and follow it.

In particular, Skinner aimed to analyze verbal events by highlighting two complementary aspects: the behavior of the speaker and the behavior of the listener. By examining these distinct perspectives, one can observe and evaluate the effects that a verbal event has on the listener, in terms of both verbal and nonverbal behaviors. Classical theories claimed that language is a sort of innate or at least developmentally driven process; in contrast, Skinner argues that language is a verbal behavior that can be better explained by the same environmental variables employed to describe any other behavior. Language is a socially meaningful behavior with high social relevance, being regulated by the interactive dynamics among individuals. In addition, language can be structured, developed, and taught by manipulating the classical environmental variables of operant conditioning (i.e., antecedent and consequent). In the behavioral analysis of language, words are not defined according to their form, but for their function (i.e., the use of variables controlling their production).

Verbal Behavior programs are important for supporting the emergence of spontaneous language, responding to questions, naming object/actions, following instructions, and utilizing visual and imitative skills.

This analysis led to the identification and framing of significant units for the study of behavior, named verbal operants (functional categories).

Each operant has its specific function, and it is controlled by specific variables.

The principal verbal operants are the following:

- *[MAND (request)]:* It is a verbal behavior controlled by states of deprivation and aversion, where its function is to request for obtaining something that is desired. This verbal operant constitutes the first and primary step in language acquisition training as it is based on the child's motivations (e.g., to request an object to obtain it). MAND generally improves language development, as through positive reinforcement granted as a consequence of the MAND itself, the child begins to associate the sound of his/her voice with a positive outcome. This verbal operant is the first one acquired by humans.
- *[ECHOIC]:* It is a verbal operant that involves imitation and repetition of a verbal behavior expressed by another person. The goal is to speak, and this must occur to be reinforced.

- *[TACT]:* It is a verbal operant that can be taught once the child has acquired a good echoic repertoire and substantial number of MANDs. It consists in naming things and/or actions that the individual comes into contact with via sensory processing.
- *[INTRAVERBAL]:* It is a type of verbal operant in which an individual responds differently to another person's verbal behavior, such as answering a question or engaging in conversation.
- *[TEXTUAL]:* It is a verbal behavior that involves reading without comprehension of the written text. Understanding the text involves the involvement of other verbal and nonverbal operants, such as intraverbal and receptive language skills (e.g., following instructions, etc.)
- *[TRANSCRIPTION]:* It involves writing a word that has been heard. Skinner refers to this operant as "dictation" because the behavior involves not only the manual production of the letters that make up the word but also accurate spelling of it.
- *[MIMETIC]:* It is sign imitation, someone's movements with a specific functional meaning are copied.

To complete it should be added that nonverbal behavior is defined as listener behavior (receptive and nonverbal), and motor actions are performed in response to what someone else has said.

Skinner also identifies secondary verbal operants: the autoclitics (adjectives, adverbs, and specifications) that add information to the primary verbal operants.

Parent-mediated intervention

Parent-mediated Communication Therapy (PACT)

PACT is an approach characterized by the direct involvement of parents or caregivers in improving the communicative abilities and social skills of children with ASD. This model is based on the idea that active parental involvement in therapy can promote children's progress and well-being. It recognizes the fundamental importance of starting from individual interests to promote interaction and learning. In supporting the acquisition of distinct skills for children with ASD, it is structured to follow the typical developmental trajectory of skills acquisition (i.e., it focuses on improving the skills of children with ASD trying to "replicate" the neurotypical developmental trajectory).

Thus, PACT should be considered a parent-mediated intervention and also an intervention for parents, and – at the same time – a naturalistic approach.

PACT is generally characterized as a parent-mediated intervention targeting preschool-aged children. In 2004, a pilot study was conducted to evaluate the putative effect of PACT methodology in combination with the treatment typically received by English children with ASD. The results seemed to be promising. PACT focuses on the most interactive and socially relevant aspects for functional communication. Thus, PACT aims at enhancing not only linguistic skills but also communicative intentionality and pragmatic competence, and this should promote the spontaneous and generalized use of communication.

Neurotypical children very early (7th–9th month) realize that their subjective contents are potentially shareable. Notably, it is during this period that intentional manifestations such as shared attention and intentions appear. For example, children can begin to point in order to direct mother's attention, and they alternate the direction of their gaze from the object to face (and vice versa). This is possible due to the myriad of previous neonatal experiences in which joint attention matched with meaningful affective exchanges (with parents and caregivers in general).

Primordial signs of joint attention may emerge very early in neurotypical development (2nd month). Joint attention is crucial to support dynamic exchange of social information, and it is a core building block of intersubjectivity. A number of studies have focused on putative anomalies in constituting and regulating joint attention mechanisms in autism, and joint attention is one of the specific targets of PACT intervention.

On one hand, PACT aims to enhance the child's communicative initiative; on the other hand, it enables parents to respond to and adapt in a way that exponentially amplifies social dynamics with their child. Parents are guided by therapists in synchronizing with their child in order to recognize his/her signals and intentions, share his/her attention, adjust to his/her timing and response modalities, reduce their intervention to promote the child's initiative, and provide contingent responses and comments related to the activity they (parents and child) are engaged in.

PACT intervention is structured into different levels that try to mirror the neurotypical developmental process (e.g., promoting shared attention; maximizing attention to linguistic inputs; promoting social routines; improving language skills, communicative functions; and, more generally, promoting communicative synchrony). Thus, PACT approach employs distinct strategies:

- *[Active parental involvement]:* Parents become a sort of "co-therapist", and they work closely with therapists to implement therapeutic strategies at home. Parents are encouraged to actively participate in therapy session and to promote skills and strategies learned during sessions also in other contexts (e.g., at home, during holidays, etc.)
- *[Promotion of reciprocal communication]:* The goal of PACT intervention is the promotion of reciprocal communication between the child and parents. This includes encouraging communicative interactions, verbal and nonverbal understanding, and the use of gestures and other forms of communication.
- *[Adaptation to the child's individual needs]:* PACT intervention adapts to the specific individual needs of each child with ASD. Therapeutic strategies are personalized to address their specific abilities, interests, and challenges.
- *[Inclusion of behavioral therapy elements]:* PACT intervention often integrates elements from behavioral therapy approaches (e.g., ABA). This means that reinforcement strategies, modeling, and environmental structuring may be used to facilitate learning and the acquisition of new skills.

PACT methodology is based on the use of video feedback as a mediation tool between the therapist and parents. Indeed, clinicians employ videos to guide parents' attention to specific aspects of their interaction with the child and to highlight effective communication strategies.

The PACT methodology is based on the need for parental mediation in the treatment, and therefore it does not require the presence of any direct intervention by the therapist (even if physically present in the room). In turn, PACT requires that parent(s) are present in every sessions. Normally, PACT consists of a relatively brief period of treatment (12 months of treatment + 6 months for supporting the conservation of results). Here again, also for PACT approach it is advisable to consult professionals specialized in the field of autism (e.g., child neuropsychiatrist and specialized therapist) to assess the specific needs and develop individualized treatment plans.

The positive effects of PACT intervention can be observed not only in a child's communicative and social skills, but also in parent–child relationship and more generally in the nuclear family quality of life. The family-centered and engaging approach promotes active parental involvement, providing them with a greater understanding of strategies and tools used during therapeutic sessions.

Psychological approaches

There are several psychological approaches that are employed in treating autism. These approaches focus on the development of social, communicative, and behavioral skills, as well as on the promotion of emotional and cognitive support for individuals with ASD.

Cognitive-Behavioral Therapy (CBT)

CBT is an approach that focuses on managing dysfunctional thoughts, emotions, and behaviors. In the context of autism, CBT can be used to address anxiety, hyperactivity, aggression, or other problematic behaviors.

CBT is a widely employed psychological approach for the treatment of autism. Although originally developed to treat mood disorders and anxiety disorders, CBT has been adapted to specifically address cognitive, behavioral, and socioemotional challenges related to autism.

CBT is based on the premise that thoughts, emotions, and behaviors are interconnected, and that changes in thinking and behaviors can positively influence mood and the overall well-being.

Concerning the domain of autism, the main goals of and specific techniques used by CBT are as follows:

- *[Anxiety management]:* CBT can help individuals with ASD to identify triggers of anxiety and to develop strategies to effectively cope with it. This may include relaxation techniques, controlled breathing, cognitive restructuring (changing negative thoughts into more positive and realistic ones), and gradual exposure to fearful situations.
- *[Reduction of problematic behaviors]:* CBT can be used to address problematic behaviors such as stereotypies, aggressive behaviors, or self-injury. This may involve identifying triggers, learning more adaptive and functional alternatives, using positive reinforcement, and modifying reward system.
- *[Development of social skills]:* CBT can be used to enhance social skills and social interactions in individuals with ASD. This may include learning conversational skills, interpretating facial expressions and nonverbal cues, identifying others' feelings, and utilizing social problem-solving strategies.
- *[Adaptation to changes and transitions]:* CBT can help individuals with ASD in effectively coping with changes in routines, transitions, and new situations. This may involve preplanning, using visual supports, modifying negative thoughts associated with change, and learning coping strategies.

CBT in the context of autism is often tailored to meet the specific cognitive and communication needs of individuals with ASD. It can be delivered individually or in a group, depending on the needs and available resources. It is important to work with a therapist experienced in autism and CBT to ensure effective and personal treatment.

Pragmatic social therapy

This therapy focuses on the development of social skills and pragmatic communication, which involves the appropriate use of language in social contexts. It works on improving conversational skills, understanding nonverbal gestures, reading others' emotions, and social rule comprehension.

Psychoeducational treatment

This approach aims to provide information and skills to individuals with ASD and their families. This should permit to better understand autism, manage problematic behaviors, cope with daily challenges, and promote independence.

Play therapy

This type of therapy is based on using play as a tool to promote social, emotional, and behavioral development. Play therapy can help children with ASD in developing social interaction skills, expressing emotions, and improving behavioral flexibility.

Family therapy

The family-centered therapeutic approach involves the active participation of family members of individuals with ASD. It focuses on emotional support, education, and management of family dynamics, aiming to create an environment supporting the growth of individuals with ASD.

Social skills training for autism

Social skills training teaches children the skills they need to interact with others. It includes repeating and reinforcing certain desired behaviors. The Children's Friendship Training intervention, for instance, helps school-aged children to improve several social skills (e.g., conversation and play together). It is important to emphasize again that every individual with ASD has specific and individual characteristics and needs. In turn, psychological approaches can be personalized based on each individual's specific needs and abilities. Some individuals may benefit from a combination of different approaches, while others may derive greater benefit from a specific approach.

Furthermore, psychological approaches in autism often involve collaboration among different professionals (e.g., psychologist, occupational therapist, speech therapist, and behavioral consultant). This multidisciplinary team works to provide comprehensive support to the individual with ASD and his/her family.

It is important to note that psychological approaches in ASD do not aim to "cure" autism, as autism is a lifelong neurodevelopmental condition with complex (and largely unknown) neurobiological underpinnings. However, they can be helpful in promoting skill development, reducing problematic behaviors, improving quality of life, and fostering social inclusion.

It is advisable to consult qualified professionals specialized in autism to assess the specific individual needs and to determine the most appropriate psychological approach. An accurate evaluation can help in identifying the specific individual challenges and to develop a personalized treatment plan.

In conclusion, psychological approaches in autism are an essential component in the treatment and support of individuals with ASD. These approaches aim to improve social, communicative, and behavioral skills while providing emotional and cognitive support. The primary goal is to promote the development and autonomy of individuals with ASD, enabling them to participate as fully as possible in social life and achieve their full potential.

Other interventions

Pharmacological treatment

Pharmacological treatment in autism can be used to address specific symptoms or comorbidities associated with autism. It is important to emphasize that there is no pharmacological cure for autism, but drugs can be used to manage certain symptoms and improve the quality of life.

Thus, the specific aims of psychopharmacological treatment can be related to both core autistic symptoms and comorbidities.

Psychopharmacological treatment should be based on accurate functional analysis in order to highlight specific symptomatic targets (e.g., hyperactivity, attention deficit, repetitive behaviors, aggressivity self-harming, destructiveness, psychomotor agitation, and social withdrawal).

Psychopharmacological treatment should be considered only after having carefully evaluated all other non-pharmacological interventions and after having considered any environmental and medical variables that may have triggered the specific symptomatic target (and also considering that these environmental and medical variables may even interact with drugs).

Pharmacological treatment in autism is generally required to manage challenging behaviors that would limit or even nullify the efficacy of non-pharmacological habilitative and rehabilitative interventions. Noteworthy, non-pharmacological interventions are crucial to maximize the possibility to limit or postpone the use of psychoactive drugs.

Dosage should be evaluated by expert physicians with caution to minimize the risk of side effects.

An important issue that should be given due attention is the safeguard of self-determination in relation to the psychoactive drug prescription.

When behavioral symptomatology is not manageable by non-pharmacological intervention, drugs can be proposed, but it should be considered that drugs may have a serious impact on individual self-determination. In addition, co-occurrence of psychopathological conditions (notably in adolescence and adulthood) in individuals with a diagnosis of ASD often risks to lead to multiple prescriptions that are generally more difficult to be monitored (in terms of efficacy and side effects).

Here, there is a list of main symptoms for which medications can be prescribed in the context of autism (note that both prescription and monitoring of medications have to be mandatorily supervised by expert physicians):

- [Hyperactivity and impulsivity]: Certain psychoactive drugs, such as stimulant medications for ADHD (e.g., methylphenidate), can be prescribed to help in reducing hyperactivity and impulsivity symptoms in individuals with ASD. These drugs can help to improve concentration, attention span, and reduce hyperactivity. However, not all individuals with ASD benefit from these drugs, and the response may vary from one person to another.
- [Behavioral problems and aggression]: In some cases, antipsychotic drugs can be used to control aggressive behaviors or severe behavioral problems that can interfere with daily life

activities. Atypical antipsychotics can be used to treat aggressive behaviors, irritability, and severe behavioral problems that can be associated with autism. These drugs can help in reducing agitation and aggression, but they should be prescribed with caution as they can have significant side effects. It is particularly important to carefully evaluate risks and benefits before initiating pharmacological treatment with antipsychotics (note that this should be a general premise for any pharmacological intervention).
- [Sleep disorders]: Some individuals with ASD may experience sleep difficulties. In such cases, short-term sedative or hypnotic drugs or supplements (e.g., melatonin) can be prescribed to promote sleep.
- [Anxiety and mood disorders]: Anxiolytic or antidepressant drugs can be prescribed if individuals with ASD experience significant anxiety or symptoms of mood disorders. In some cases, anxiolytic or antidepressant drugs can be prescribed to alleviate these symptoms. However, it is important to note that the use of these drugs should be closely monitored as they can have side effects and pharmacological interactions (note that this should be a general premise for any pharmacological intervention or supplements prescription).
- [Epilepsy]: Epilepsy is relatively a common comorbidity in autism. Thus, it is crucial to consider it both during the diagnostic process and during the setting of treatment. A greater prevalence of epilepsy is reported in adults with ASD than in children with ASD, and a greater prevalence in adolescents with ASD than in school-aged children with ASD.
- [Gastrointestinal disorders]: Some individuals with ASD may suffer from gastrointestinal disorders, such as gastroesophageal reflux disease or irritable bowel syndrome. In some cases, drugs can be prescribed to manage these symptoms.

It is important to note that the decision to use drugs in the treatment of autism should be made in collaboration with a specialized medical professional, such as a child neuropsychiatrist or psychiatrist, who will carefully assess the benefits and potential side effects of drugs. Each individual with autism is unique, and the response to drugs can vary; therefore, pharmacological treatment should be personalized based on the specific needs and general clinical condition of each individual.

Furthermore, it is essential to emphasize that pharmacological treatment should always be integrated with behavioral interventions, educational approaches, and specific therapies for autism, which represent the primary approach to promote the development and overall well-being of individuals with ASD. The use of drugs in the treatment of autism is a complex decision that needs to be evaluated on a case-by-case basis, carefully considering specific symptoms, individual needs, and potential side effects of drugs. It is important to work in collaboration with a specialized physician experienced in autism to ensure accurate assessment and appropriate medication management.

The main goal in treating autism is to provide a comprehensive approach that takes into account individual needs and promotes overall well-being. This may involve a combination of drugs, behavioral therapies, educational interventions, family support, and other complementary therapies such as occupational therapy and speech therapy.

It is important to remember that autism is a complex disorder and individual responses to drugs can vary. This means that drugs can be effective for some individuals but not for others. It is crucial to carefully evaluate the potential benefits and side effects of drugs and constantly monitor individual response (and here again, we stress the need that this should be done by expert physicians).

Finally, the treatment of autism should be personalized and tailored to the specific needs of each individual. It is advisable to consult with a professional experienced in the field of autism and work closely with a multidisciplinary team to ensure a comprehensive and integrated approach in the treatment of autism.

Nutritional therapy for autism

Many types of diets or supplements have been suggested as treatments for autism. However, these recommendations are not supported by international scientific evidence. The use of specific diets is based on empirical observations that cannot be generalized to autism, and they are derived from a limited number of "single case studies" (which is obviously not a reliable approach from a methodological point of view). Nonetheless, there is scientific evidence indicating a significant presence of atypical eating behaviors and/or gastrointestinal disorders in children with ASD.

For a variety of reasons, often children with ASD do not get the nutrition they need for a healthy growth and development. Some children with ASD only eat certain foods because of the foods' taste they feel in their mouths. Other times, they may avoid foods because they associate them with stomach pain or discomfort. It is very important that parents and caregivers work with a nutrition specialist – such as a registered dietitian or a medical doctor or other recognized healthcare providers – to design a meal plan for a person with ASD, especially if they want to try a limited diet. Such nutrition specialists can help to assure that the child is still getting all the nutrients that he/she needs to grow in a healthy way. For example, several children with ASD are on gluten-free or casein-free diets. To date, scientific evidence does not support the "by-default use" of a casein-free diet or the use of gluten-free diet, or the "by-default use" of a combined gluten-free + casein-free diet as a treatment for individuals with ASD (for sure, these specific diets have to be prescribed – here again, only by expert medical doctors after accurate diagnostic process – in cases of autistic individuals with real celiac disease).

Generally speaking, a good nutrition is important: research studies indicate that children with ASD tend to have thinner bones than typically developing children. Restricting access to bone-building foods, such as dairy products, can make it even harder for their bones to grow strong.

Working with a nutrition specialist (e.g., registered dietitian, medical doctor, and other recognized healthcare providers) can help ensure that children who are on special diets still get the bone-building and other nutrients they need.

Some people with ASD also have digestive problems, such as constipation, abdominal pain, or vomiting. Some studies suggest that digestive problems occur more often in people with ASD, but further research is needed to confirm or confute such a hypothesis. Working with a nutrition specialist can help ensure that a diet does not make digestive problems worse.

A general conclusive consideration is that any nutritional choice (e.g., any diet) is an important issue that deserves serious attention, and support by experts (e.g., physicians, neuropsychiatrists, etc.). Self-prescription can be very counter-productive and even very dangerous.

Ethical considerations concerning the choice and management of treatment

Ethical and legal aspects in the treatment of autism play a fundamental role in ensuring adequate care and protection for the rights of individuals with ASD. It is important to consider the following points:

- [Informed consent]: Before starting any treatment, it is necessary to obtain informed consent from parents or legal guardians. This assures that they can have clear and comprehensive information regarding potential benefits, risks, and alternatives of a specific treatment, supporting them in making a well-informed decision.
- [Patient rights and well-being]: In the treatment of autism, patients' rights and well-being must be considered a priority. This entails the adoption of a person-centered approach, respecting the dignity, autonomy, and self-determination of individuals with ASD. It is important to ensure that treatment decisions are made in their best interest.
- [Evidence-based therapies]: Therapies and interventions used in the treatment of autism should be based on scientific evidence. It is important for professionals to follow recognized guidelines and use validated therapeutic approaches that have demonstrated efficacy in improving outcomes for individuals with ASD.
- [Respect for diversity and inclusion]: In the treatment of ASD, it is essential to adopt an approach that respects diversity and promotes social inclusion. This is particularly important considering specific individual needs and preferences, as well as the values and perspectives of individuals with ASD and their families.

- [Privacy and confidentiality]: In the treatment of autism, it is crucial to protect the privacy and confidentiality of individuals' personal information. Professionals must adhere to privacy regulations and obtain consent for the disclosure of personal information, ensuring that such information is treated securely and confidentially.
- [Teamwork and collaboration]: In the treatment of autism, teamwork and collaboration are essential. Professionals must work in collaboration with parents, guardians, and other members of the multidisciplinary team to ensure coordinated and integrated care, sharing information and making joint decisions for the patients' well-being.
- [Legal responsibility]: Professionals providing treatments for autism must be aware of the laws and regulations in force in their country or region. They must adhere to professional standards, practice according to ethical guidelines, and have legal responsibility in providing adequate and safe treatment.

In conclusion, the treatment of autism requires an ethical approach that respects the rights of individuals with ASD. It is essential to ensure fair, evidence-based, and patient-centered treatment while respecting the rights, diversity, and inclusion of individuals with ASD. Ethical and legal aspects in the treatment of autism not only safeguard patients but also contribute to promote the quality of care.

It is important to stay updated on new scientific discoveries and best practices in the treatment of autism, as the understanding of this disorder is constantly evolving. Generally speaking, this is always important; however, it is particularly important and mandatory for aspects such as pharmacological intervention and nutritional aspects (considering rapid advancements in research that necessarily imply strict medical supervision). Maintaining high professional ethics and adhering to the principles of responsibility and integrity are essential to ensure adequate and highly qualitative treatment for individuals with ASD.

The ethical and legal aspects in the treatment of autism may vary from one country to another and may change over time. Therefore, it is advisable to consult relevant local news, regulations, and guidelines, and to collaborate with experienced and qualified professionals in the field of autism to ensure ethically and legally compliant treatments.

Bibliography

Aldred, C., Green, J., & Adams, C. (2004). A new social communication intervention for children with autism: Pilot randomised controlled treatment study suggesting effectiveness. *Journal of Child Psychology and Psychiatry, and Allied Disciplines*, 45(8), 1420–1430.

Aman, M. G., McDougle, C. J., Scahill, L., Handen, B., Arnold, L. E., Johnson, C., Stigler, K. A., Bearss, K., Butter, E., Swiezy, N. B., Sukhodolsky, D. D., Ramadan, Y., Pozdol, S. L., Nikolov, R., Lecavalier, L., Kohn, A. E., Koenig, K., Hollway, J. A., Korzekwa, P., Gavaletz, A., ... Research Units on Pediatric Psychopharmacology Autism Network (2009). Medication and parent training in children with pervasive developmental disorders and serious behavior problems: Results from a randomized clinical trial. *Journal of the American Academy of Child and Adolescent Psychiatry*, 48(12), 1143–1154.

Bondy, A., & Frost, L. (2001). The picture exchange communication system. *Behavior Modification*, 25(5), 725–744.

Bondy, A., Tincani, M., & Frost, L. (2004). Multiply controlled verbal operants: An analysis and extension to the picture exchange communication system. *The Behavior Analyst*, 27(2), 247–261.

Buie, T., Campbell, D. B., Fuchs, G. J., 3rd, Furuta, G. T., Levy, J., Vandewater, J., Whitaker, A. H., Atkins, D., Bauman, M. L., Beaudet, A. L., Carr, E. G., Gershon, M. D., Hyman, S. L., Jirapinyo, P., Jyonouchi, H., Kooros, K., Kushak, R., Levitt, P., Levy, S. E., Lewis, J. D., ... Winter, H. (2010). Evaluation, diagnosis, and treatment of gastrointestinal disorders in individuals with ASDs: A consensus report. *Pediatrics*, 125 (Suppl 1), S1–S18.

Chaidez, V., Hansen, R. L., & Hertz-Picciotto, I. (2014). Gastrointestinal problems in children with autism, developmental delays or typical development. *Journal of Autism and Developmental Disorders*, 44(5), 1117–1127.

Chang, Y. C., Shire, S. Y., Shih, W., Gelfand, C., & Kasari, C. (2016). Preschool deployment of evidence-based social communication intervention: JASPER in the classroom. *Journal of Autism and Developmental Disorders*, 46(6), 2211–2223.

Charlop-Christy, M. H., Carpenter, M., Le, L., LeBlanc, L. A., & Kellet, K. (2002). Using the Picture Exchange Communication System (PECS) with children with autism: Assessment of PECS acquisition, speech, social-communicative behavior, and problem behavior. *Journal of Applied Behavior Analysis*, 35(3), 213–231.

Dawson G. (2008). Early behavioral intervention, brain plasticity, and the prevention of autism spectrum disorder. *Development and Psychopathology*, 20(3), 775–803.

Dawson, G., Jones, E. J., Merkle, K., Venema, K., Lowy, R., Faja, S., Kamara, D., Murias, M., Greenson, J., Winter, J., Smith, M., Rogers, S. J., & Webb, S. J. (2012). Early behavioral intervention is associated with normalized brain activity in young children with autism. *Journal of the American Academy of Child and Adolescent Psychiatry*, 51(11), 1150–1159.

Dawson, G., Rogers, S., Munson, J., Smith, M., Winter, J., Greenson, J., Donaldson, A., & Varley, J. (2010). Randomized, controlled trial of an intervention for toddlers with autism: The Early Start Denver Model. *Pediatrics*, 125(1), e17–e23.

Ganz, J. B., & Simpson, R. L. (2004). Effects on communicative requesting and speech development of the Picture Exchange Communication System in children with characteristics of autism. *Journal of Autism and Developmental Disorders*, 34(4), 395–409.

Green, J., Charman, T., McConachie, H., Aldred, C., Slonims, V., Howlin, P., Le Couteur, A., Leadbitter, K., Hudry, K., Byford, S., Barrett, B., Temple, K., Macdonald, W., Pickles, A., & PACT Consortium (2010). Parent-mediated communication-focused treatment in children with autism (PACT): A randomised controlled trial. *Lancet (London, England)*, 375(9732), 2152–2160.

Green, J., Leadbitter, K., Ellis, C., Taylor, L., Moore, H. L., Carruthers, S., ... & Pickles, A. (2022). Combined social communication therapy at home and in education for young autistic children in England (PACT-G): A parallel, single-blind, randomised controlled trial. *The Lancet Psychiatry*, 9(4), 307–320.

Hediger, M. L., England, L. J., Molloy, C. A., Yu, K. F., Manning-Courtney, P., & Mills, J. L. (2008). Reduced bone cortical thickness in boys with autism or autism spectrum disorder. *Journal of Autism and Developmental Disorders*, 38(5), 848–856.

Handen, B. L., Johnson, C. R., & Lubetsky, M. (2000). Efficacy of methylphenidate among children with autism and symptoms of attention-deficit hyperactivity disorder. *Journal of Autism and Developmental Disorders*, 30(3), 245–255.

Helt, M., Kelley, E., Kinsbourne, M., Pandey, J., Boorstein, H., Herbert, M., & Fein, D. (2008). Can children with autism recover? If so, how?. *Neuropsychology Review*, 18(4), 339–366.

Herndon, A. C., DiGuiseppi, C., Johnson, S. L., Leiferman, J., & Reynolds, A. (2009). Does nutritional intake differ between children with autism spectrum disorders and children with typical development?. *Journal of Autism and Developmental Disorders*, 39(2), 212–222.

Johnson, C. P., Myers, S. M., & American Academy of Pediatrics Council on Children with Disabilities (2007). Identification and evaluation of children with autism spectrum disorders. *Pediatrics*, 120(5), 1183–1215.

Kasari, C., Gulsrud, A., Paparella, T., Hellemann, G., & Berry, K. (2015). Randomized comparative efficacy study of parent-mediated interventions for toddlers with autism. *Journal of Consulting and Clinical Psychology*, 83(3), 554–563.

Kasari, C., Lawton, K., Shih, W., Barker, T. V., Landa, R., Lord, C., Orlich, F., King, B., Wetherby, A., & Senturk, D. (2014). Caregiver-mediated intervention for low-resourced preschoolers with autism: An RCT. *Pediatrics*, 134(1), e72–e79.

Keel, J. H., Mesibov, G. B., & Woods, A. V. (1997). TEACCH-supported employment program. *Journal of Autism and Developmental Disorders*, 27(1), 3–9.

Kurz, R., Huemer, J., Muchitsch, E., & Feucht, M. (2018). Cognitive behavioral therapy for children with autism spectrum disorder: A prospective observational study. *European Journal of Paediatric Neurology: EJPN: Official Journal of the European Paediatric Neurology Society*, 22(5), 803–806.

Lang, R., Hancock, T. B., & Singh, N. N. (Eds.). (2016). *Early intervention for young children with autism spectrum disorder*. Springer.

Lei, J., & Ventola, P. (2017). Pivotal response treatment for autism spectrum disorder: Current perspectives. *Neuropsychiatric Disease and Treatment*, 13, 1613–1626.

Lord, C., Charman, T., Havdahl, A., Carbone, P., Anagnostou, E., Boyd, B., Carr, T., de Vries, P. J., Dissanayake, C., Divan, G., Freitag, C. M., Gotelli, M. M., Kasari, C., Knapp, M., Mundy, P., Plank, A., Scahill, L., Servili, C., Shattuck, P., Simonoff, E., ... McCauley, J. B. (2022). The Lancet Commission on the future of care and clinical research in autism. *Lancet (London, England)*, 399(10321), 271–334.

Marcus, R. N., Owen, R., Manos, G., Mankoski, R., Kamen, L., McQuade, R. D., Carson, W. H., & Findling, R. L. (2011). Safety and tolerability of aripiprazole for irritability in pediatric patients with autistic disorder: A 52-week, open-label, multicenter study. *The Journal of Clinical Psychiatry*, 72(9), 1270–1276.

McConachie, H., & Diggle, T. (2007). Parent implemented early intervention for young children with autism spectrum disorder: A systematic review. *Journal of Evaluation in Clinical Practice*, 13(1), 120–129.

McCracken, J. T., McGough, J., Shah, B., Cronin, P., Hong, D., Aman, M. G., Arnold, L. E., Lindsay, R., Nash, P., Hollway, J., McDougle, C. J., Posey, D., Swiezy, N., Kohn, A., Scahill, L., Martin, A., Koenig, K., Volkmar, F., Carroll, D., Lancor, A., ... Research Units on Pediatric Psychopharmacology Autism Network (2002). Risperidone in children with autism and serious behavioral problems. *The New England Journal of Medicine*, 347(5), 314–321.

McDaniel, J., Yoder, P., Crandall, M., Millan, M. E., Ardel, C. M., Gengoux, G. W., & Hardan, A. Y. (2020). Effects of pivotal response treatment on reciprocal vocal contingency in a randomized controlled trial of children with autism spectrum disorder. *Autism: The International Journal of Research and Practice*, 24(6), 1566–1571.

Mesibov, G. B., & Shea, V. (2010). The TEACCH program in the era of evidence-based practice. *Journal of Autism and Developmental Disorders*, 40(5), 570–579.

Mohammadzaheri, F., Koegel, L. K., Rezaee, M., & Rafiee, S. M. (2014). A randomized clinical trial comparison between pivotal response treatment (PRT) and structured applied behavior analysis (ABA) intervention for children with autism. *Journal of Autism and Developmental Disorders*, 44(11), 2769–2777.

Pickles, A., Le Couteur, A., Leadbitter, K., Salomone, E., Cole-Fletcher, R., Tobin, H., Gammer, I., Lowry, J., Vamvakas, G., Byford, S., Aldred, C., Slonims, V., McConachie, H., Howlin, P., Parr, J. R., Charman, T., & Green, J. (2016). Parent-mediated social communication therapy for young children with autism (PACT): Long-term follow-up of a randomised controlled trial. *Lancet (London, England)*, 388(10059), 2501–2509.

Reichow, B., & Wolery, M. (2009). Comprehensive synthesis of early intensive behavioral interventions for young children with autism based on the UCLA young autism project model. *Journal of Autism and Developmental Disorders*, 39(1), 23–41.

Rogers, S. J., Estes, A., Lord, C., Munson, J., Rocha, M., Winter, J., Greenson, J., Colombi, C., Dawson, G., Vismara, L. A., Sugar, C. A., Hellemann, G., Whelan, F., & Talbott, M. (2019). A multisite randomized controlled two-phase trial of the Early Start Denver Model compared to Treatment as Usual. *Journal of the American Academy of Child and Adolescent Psychiatry*, 58(9), 853–865.

Rogers, S. J., Estes, A., Lord, C., Vismara, L., Winter, J., Fitzpatrick, A., Guo, M., & Dawson, G. (2012). Effects of a brief Early Start Denver Model (ESDM)-based parent intervention on toddlers at risk for autism spectrum disorders: A randomized controlled trial. *Journal of the American Academy of Child and Adolescent Psychiatry*, 51(10), 1052–1065.

Schwartzman, J. M., Strong, K., Ardel, C. M., Schuck, R. K., Millan, M. E., Phillips, J. M., Hardan, A. Y., & Gengoux, G. W. (2021). Language improvement following pivotal response treatment for children with developmental disorders. *American Journal on Intellectual and Developmental Disabilities*, 126(1), 45–57.

Shire, S. Y., Shih, W., Chang, Y. C., Bracaglia, S., Kodjoe, M., & Kasari, C. (2019). Sustained community implementation of JASPER intervention with toddlers with autism. *Journal of Autism and Developmental Disorders*, 49(5), 1863–1875.

Ventola, P. E., Oosting, D. R., Keifer, C. M., & Friedman, H. E. (2015). Toward optimal outcome following pivotal response treatment: A case series. *The Yale Journal of Biology and Medicine*, 88(1), 37–44.

Verschuur, R., Huskens, B., Korzilius, H., Bakker, L., Snijder, M., & Didden, R. (2020). Pivotal response treatment: A study into the relationship between therapist characteristics and fidelity of implementation. *Autism: The International Journal of Research and Practice*, 24(2), 499–514.

Virues-Ortega, J., Julio, F. M., & Pastor-Barriuso, R. (2013). The TEACCH program for children and adults with autism: A meta-analysis of intervention studies. *Clinical Psychology Review*, 33(8), 940–953.

Wang, X., Zhao, J., Huang, S., Chen, S., Zhou, T., Li, Q., Luo, X., & Hao, Y. (2021). Cognitive behavioral therapy for autism spectrum disorders: A systematic review. *Pediatrics*, 147(5), e2020049880.

Wong, C., & Kasari, C. (2012). Play and joint attention of children with autism in the preschool special education classroom. *Journal of Autism and Developmental Disorders*, 42(10), 2152–2161.

Wood, J. J., Drahota, A., Sze, K., Har, K., Chiu, A., & Langer, D. A. (2009). Cognitive behavioral therapy for anxiety in children with autism spectrum disorders: A randomized, controlled trial. *Journal of Child Psychology and Psychiatry, and Allied Disciplines*, 50(3), 224–234.

Wood, J. J., Ehrenreich-May, J., Alessandri, M., Fujii, C., Renno, P., Laugeson, E., Piacentini, J. C., De Nadai, A. S., Arnold, E., Lewin, A. B., Murphy, T. K., & Storch, E. A. (2015). Cognitive behavioral therapy for early adolescents with autism spectrum disorders and clinical anxiety: A randomized, controlled trial. *Behavior Therapy*, 46(1), 7–19.

Wood, J. J., Kendall, P. C., Wood, K. S., Kerns, C. M., Seltzer, M., Small, B. J., Lewin, A. B., & Storch, E. A. (2020). Cognitive behavioral treatments for anxiety in children with autism spectrum disorder: A randomized clinical trial. *JAMA Psychiatry*, 77(5), 474–483.

Zimmer, M. H., Hart, L. C., Manning-Courtney, P., Murray, D. S., Bing, N. M., & Summer, S. (2012). Food variety as a predictor of nutritional status among children with autism. *Journal of Autism and Developmental Disorders*, 42(4), 549–556.

Zwaigenbaum, L., Bauman, M. L., Choueiri, R., Kasari, C., Carter, A., Granpeesheh, D., Mailloux, Z., Smith Roley, S., Wagner, S., Fein, D., Pierce, K., Buie, T., Davis, P. A., Newschaffer, C., Robins, D., Wetherby, A., Stone, W. L., Yirmiya, N., Estes, A., Hansen, R. L., ... Natowicz, M. R. (2015). Early intervention for children with autism spectrum disorder under 3 years of age: Recommendations for practice and research. *Pediatrics*, 136(Suppl 1), S60–S81.

Chapter 5

Autism Spectrum Disorder
Positive Prognosis, Optimal Outcome, Best *Feasible* Outcome, and Recovery

Laura Villa

From diagnosis to prognosis

It is not trivial to reply to questions concerning prognosis following a diagnosis of ASD. First, autism is characterized by multiple and heterogeneous developmental trajectories; in addition, to date any index reported in the literature as associated with favorable prognosis is generic, then it remains far to be understood with high standard of scientific methodology which elements should be considered as a positive (or a negative) prognostic factor. Obviously, the lack of a clear conclusion in the literature is not simplistic due to the lack of rigor in designing studies. There are objective difficulties in designing robust and well-controlled studies to address such a point.

Considerable complexity in establishing clear scenarios for positive versus negative prognosis is related to the interaction between genetic and epigenetic factors impacting developmental trajectories. Epigenetics refer to any environmental factors that interact with the individual genetic profile, and normally also habilitative and rehabilitative programs are considered epigenetic protective factors. Thus, if clinical programs have a significant impact on the prognosis of autism, it is clearly reasonable that parent(s) ask about the efficacy of treatments, and which one may more positively impact their child's prognosis, quality of life, and more generally his/her future.

It is essential to consider how and how much the future can eventually be influenced by interventions planned after the diagnosis.

To support families dealing with this uncertainty implies a prognostic view that it is not grounded exclusively on the presence and absence of specific positive or negative factors; in contrast, the prognostic view should be grounded on the peculiarities of each individual and on his/her derailed developmental trajectories that are (bi-directionally) influenced by the rehabilitative environment, by the habilitative opportunities, and by the extended family's engagement.

Indeed, as normally happens in medicine, prognosis is conditioned also by the contribution of the clinical intervention.

When parent(s) wonder about prognosis, their interest concerns a multi-level range of questions. Indeed, they manifest not only specific requests concerning short-term prognosis (e.g., "what about the consequences if we undertake this or the other rehabilitative intervention?"), but also regarding long-term prognosis. They are interested in understanding the possibility of (very) positive prognosis, or even they wonder whether the very positive prognosis may correspond to an effective recovery. They often have pragmatical examples in mind, such as "will he/she have a job in the future?", or "will he/she be able to have an independent life?", or "will he/she be able to be engaged in a romantic relationship?".

In the literature, from the one side following rehabilitative intervention, potential positive and promising developmental trajectories have been described; from the other side, even in these cases residual symptomology can persist, and it should be attentively taken into account considering that it may have a non-marginal impact on the quality of life and on the need of long-term clinical support.

In addition, during development autism may be complicated by potential comorbidities with other medical and psychopathological conditions that may undermine the balance previously achieved.

Thus, although the picture is complex, age-dependent, and cannot be simplistically reduced to a short summary, it is important to provide some hints concerning short-, medium-, and long-term prognosis.

Prognosis and potential outcome(s)

In the literature, we can find different terms employed to putatively map a positive developmental trajectory: "good outcome", "best outcome", and "optimal outcome" are broad constructs that may help in orienting both expectations and goals. In addition, also the term "recovery" is employed in the context of autism, although it should not be considered simplistically as a medical recovery (e.g., a "full recovery" from an infection). Noteworthy, to state that recovery in autism does not coincide with the classical idea of medical recovery does not mean that favorable results in autism are impossible, or even that any victory should be considered – to some extent – as an illusory victory.

Thus, positive prognosis is described in the literature with different terms: "best outcome" and "optimal outcome" can be considered as synonymous. These constructs are generally employed to map a positive result that it is not enough for retracting the diagnosis of ASD. In contrast, "recovery" is often employed to indicate the lack of diagnostic confirmation of ASD.

Therefore, positive prognosis is described in a heterogeneous and often inconsistent way: this inconsistency induces families in hoping for a recovery interpreted not only as the lack of diagnostic confirmation of ASD, but often surreptitiously it suggests the idea of "full recovery" (similarly to the recovery from an infection). This is a misleading and often counter-productive illusion. "Optimal outcome" should effectively map the best *feasible* outcome, without confusing it with the utopian idea of the "disappearance" of ASD (i.e., "full recovery").

Families should be supported in following their child's developmental trajectories changes, in trying to map the evolution of his/her peculiar functioning or variations of behavior; in other words, parent(s) should be encouraged to be focused on the functional diagnosis instead of the categorical diagnosis (that remains normally stable across time).

Any child manifests a peculiar profile of (atypical) functioning, with specific adaptive abilities, recovery time, and generalization abilities; some children show slow but constant growth curves, whereas others show irregular and unstable curves; some children are able to acquire new competencies alone, whereas others need constant support and tutorship, or even certain children may also show excellent (extraordinary) abilities.

Thus, next to the idea that autistic phenotypical manifestations are age-dependent, an additional aspect should be underlined: rehabilitative outcomes should be considered making reference to specific, atypical, and derailed developmental trajectories of individuals with ASD.

In autism, developmental trajectories result from specific abilities (e.g., linguistic, cognitive, motor, etc.) that progress according to a peculiar chronology; such an atypical chronology may slow down or speed up the developmental milestones usually reported in neurotypical individuals.

Notably, the main factor characterizing autism as a neurodevelopmental disorder is the peculiar "atypicality" of developmental trajectories. Any ability has a specific trajectory and its specific outcome, and this is the idea behind our use of the term "development".

In neurotypical individuals, developmental trajectories proceed with regular and generally replicable patterns; in contrast, developmental trajectories in autism are far to be homogeneous and predictable, with high inter-individual differences. In turn, considering that in autism complex abilities may sometimes be acquired before easier ones, in autism it can be difficult to clearly identify developmental trajectories according to clear developmental milestones.

By now, the question can be: which is the "right" form of "optimal outcome" that should be considered in the context of autism? A comprehensive ("all inclusive") "optimal outcome" composed by the summation of multiple abilities, or a more detailed ("unpacked") "optimal outcome" reflecting one specific ability? Should we consider the "optimal outcome" of a specific aspect (e.g., social play and pattern of interests) or a more general "optimal outcome" referring to broader and more complex constructs (e.g., adaptive skills and quality of life)?

In the literature, two putative temporal windows are reported suggesting the possibility of recovery from the diagnosis: the first one is around 4–5 years old and the second one is around 7–8 years old. The first one would mainly include children that received early diagnosis and early intervention, without intellectual disability; the second one would include children that received the diagnosis later, and again without intellectual disability (i.e., the so-called "high-functioning" group that mainly received diagnosis of ASD following the observation of socio-communicative difficulties).

Here, we are touching a crucial and challenging point: is it reasonable to speak about "recovery" when one individual has gained considerable adaptive and socio-communicate skills even if the diagnosis of ASD is still present? Should we embrace the idea that a detailed analysis of autistic phenotypical manifestations forces us to focus on the functional diagnosis (that would outdo categorical diagnosis)? Considering that functional diagnosis is grounded on atypical phenotypical manifestations, in cases in which these atypical phenotypical manifestations are no more observable (through gold-standard diagnostic tests) should we question even the categorical diagnosis (i.e., the label "ASD")? This is the crucial and challenging point.

The point should be analyzed in depth: if one hypothesizes that the functional diagnosis grounded on phenotypical manifestations has not a specific neurobiological counterpart, then the lack of phenotypical manifestations (i.e., atypical behaviors are no more observable through gold-standard methods) should imply the concept of "full recovery". However, there is consistent evidence in the literature ascertaining specific (even if largely unknown) neurobiological counterparts of ASD that remain "beyond" the lack of phenotypical manifestations; in turn, according to such evidence, the possibility of "full recovery" should be excluded (i.e., the concept of "recovery" for ASD is not comparable to the medical recovery from an infection).

Thus, the point would be to consider the idiographic diagnosis grounded on the specific individual functioning, and no more the nosographic diagnosis (based on the categorical label).

In other words, we could say that even if an individual with ASD is not manifesting it anymore (i.e., he/she has no more the peculiar phenotypical manifestations usually reported in individuals with ASD), the core neurobiological substrate that the scientific literature ascribed to ASD – to some extent – persists.

To challenge this issue trying to find reasonable guidelines would support the value of the functional diagnosis beyond the oversimplistic and taken-for-granted faith in categorical diagnosis.

In any case, factors that have been related to positive prognosis remain – until now – rather generic in the literature.

For example, the presence of a second co-diagnosis of a different neurodevelopmental disorder (e.g., ADHD, language disorder, intellectual disability, etc.) can have an unfavorable influence on the prognosis, as well as the presence of significant levels of core autistic symptoms (e.g., restrict and repetitive behaviors and frequency of motor stereotypies). Their presence would indicate a specific subgroup of individuals with less positive prognosis. Noteworthy, these data should not be considered as a verdict without appeal; they are important and generally reliable at the "group level" (i.e., "normally it happens that…") but they have not the same value at the level of one specific individual person. This means that it may happen that even an individual with ASD with additional risk factors (e.g., language delay) will have a positive outcome.

Optimal outcome: how and when?

Beyond our focus on potential multiple meanings and nuances that the construct of "outcome" may entail, there is a general definition reported in the literature for the term "optimal outcome", and it is the one associated with the idea of "functional recovery". To fulfil the definition of "functional recovery" (i.e., a recovery that concerns phenotypical manifestations), a number of conditions should be satisfied:

- An individual should have a previous diagnosis of ASD.
- An individual should be able to learn and use his/her learning abilities in a manner comparable to neurotypical peers.
- An individual does not meet anymore the criteria for the DSM-5-based diagnosis of ASD.

In addition, recent research has also underlined additional conditions:

- An individual does not present social functioning or communication difficulties (as screened by the ADOS).

- An individual does not participate in any specific rehabilitative protocol for autism (if he/she participates in any rehabilitative program, it should be for difficulties non-specifically ascribable to the core autistic phenotype, e.g., language).
- An individual does not need specific support at school.
- An individual should have the IQ level in the normal range.
- An individual should be in the normal range concerning adaptive skills as screened by the Vineland scale (communication and socialization).

A crucial component of such a definition of "optimal outcome" resulting in "functional recovery" is that it does not limit to core DSM-5 symptomatology for ASD, whereas it considers also broader areas of functional development. This point is important because it prevents to use the term "functional recovery" when rehabilitative programs have "just" reduced symptoms without clear, robust, and widespread changes concerning the individual functioning and adaptative skills.

Recent reviews in the literature have explored the topic trying to indicate the percentage of individuals that may fulfill the criteria for "functional recovery". However, an obvious difficulty concerns the extreme variability of factors co-influencing the prognosis (e.g., IQ, language level, verbal and motor imitation, age of diagnosis, comorbidities, and socio-economics factors). In addition, a major source of inconsistency also regards the interaction of these factors. Normally a single factor is not enough to support a reliable prediction concerning potential "functional recovery". The problem is that combining them from the one side complicates any experimental design and risks to create models that make sense only for one specific individual; from the other side, the combined analysis of these factors is the only way to provide a reliable prediction.

Early interventions are considered useful and promising, and a specific neurobiological argument supports such a statement: the central nervous system is extremely plastic, notably in early developmental stages. Neuroplasticity is particularly important in specific pre- and perinatal critical developmental windows in which neural architecture is establishing. This further supports the relevance of early diagnosis and intervention in the context of autism.

Accordingly, early intervention represents an additional crucial factor in supporting positive prognosis, and this further ascertains that rehabilitative outcomes result from complex and multilayered interactions of multiple factors (e.g., neurobiological, epigenetic, contextual, individual, etc.).

Optimal outcome: residual manifestations

A further very important point should be considered: even in cases in which "functional recovery" is reached and there are positive prognostic factors such as good cognitive functioning, there may persist subtler difficulties in social functioning and persistent (even if more nuanced) restrictive and repetitive patterns of behaviors. Consequently, neither "optimal outcome" nor "optimal outcome resulting in functional recovery" can be simplistically considered as a "full recovery", whereas they should more appropriately be considered as the best *feasible* outcome for that specific individual (and this best *feasible* outcome has significantly improved his/her adaptive skills and reduced the impact of autistic phenotypical manifestations on his/her distinct developmental stages).

Taken together, all these considerations strongly suggest that positive prognosis cannot be considered a monolithic, rigid, and immutable construct. Positive prognosis is age-dependent, co-diagnosis dependent, and context-dependent. Notably, from childhood to adulthood individuals with ASD have to face a number of challenges. From medical (e.g., epilepsy, immune system disorders, etc.) to psychiatric (e.g., anxiety) domains, a number of conditions have been found to co-occur with ASD. For example, ADHD is a common comorbidity reported in adults with ASD, and it has significant impacts on executive functions, on relationships with peers, and, more generally, on the quality of life. In addition, in the literature there are cases in which problems with substance of abuse, problems in managing and regulating sexuality, or problems of bullying have been reported.

Thus, what is the right way to consider outcomes in the context of ASD? Should we consider outcomes as age-dependent?

Should we consider a "global" outcome or should we consider an outcome as the result of a specific developmental trajectory of one specific ability? What are the risk factors in each specific developmental period? What are the protective factors?

Certain scholars have identified three "barriers" for individuals with ASD during the transition to adulthood: first, poor adaptation to the environment, that is, the lack of correspondence among the unique needs expressed by individuals with ASD and the opportunities given from specific environment (e.g., individuals with ASD's peculiar abilities are often underestimated in the work environment); second, uncertainty concerning parental role in supporting the transition to adulthood (e.g., many parents hope for their daughter's/son's greater autonomy, but finally they have hard time in actively supporting such an increased autonomy because they persist in doing daily life activities for them); and, third, the lack of efficient and widespread services for supporting such a transition. In parallel, there are also factors described in the literature that may provide support during the transition to adulthood – for example, the presence of specifically individualized programs or environmental changes (e.g., concerning sensory environment, concerning the presence of a specific caregiver that provides support in managing the relationships on the workplace, etc.). An additional important positive element regards the possibility that services and employers may receive a detailed description of the specific peculiarities such as abilities and limitations, needs, and clinical history (e.g., sensory functioning, previous rehabilitative and pharmacological history, etc.) of each individual with ASD. Noteworthy, also the possibility that individuals with ASD have access to contexts and experiences appropriate for their age may help in reducing their anxiety concerning the transition.

This means that outcomes are strictly related not only to transitions across ages but also to the congruity of services that should reflect the evolution of specific competences (i.e., it is crucial to avoid services that do not take into account the age-dependent peculiarities and specificities of autism).

A certain number of studies have tried to analyze this complex set of issues. Some of them tried to map specific clinical parameters that can potentially predict positive prognosis; however, as widely argued in this chapter, it is extremely difficult to focus on a specific predictor considering that any phenotypical marker is strongly influenced both by individual development (i.e., it is age-dependent) and by the volatility of the context (i.e., it is context-dependent).

Furthermore, additional studies focus on a sort of residual symptomatology that normally gets away from the templates of classical clinical tests employed to support categorical diagnosis. Rigorous assessment of the potential impact of residual symptomatology on an individual's adaptive skill is crucial to corroborate the "real" residuality of the disorder; this certifies again the need of considering rigorously developmental trajectories grouping homogeneous individuals (both from the perspective of initial functioning and the functioning after rehabilitative/habilitative treatments). More simply, the fact that classical clinical tests are no more certifying signs of difficulties (e.g., in social functioning, in communication, etc.) does not mean that there does not persist subtle residual deficit even in individuals that are considered with "optimal outcome resulting in functional recovery". A number of additional clinical tests are potentially available for identifying even subtler residual difficulties. For example, ADOS or Vineland are not always enough to detect subtler residual difficulties; clinical tests capable of screening the quality of friendship and peer interactions in a finely nuanced way – e.g., in more ecological settings – should be considered (when available) or created (when not available).

An additional caveat may be represented by the fact that normally there is not any specific analysis of potential disparities among different familiar contributions in supporting individuals with ASD.

In the literature, parent(s) of individuals grouped into the "optimal outcome" subgroup are generally highly engaged in rehabilitative programs. Parent(s) who actively support both rehabilitative and habilitative programs, and who proactively try to transfer and generalize trainings also in the daily life contexts (e.g., family, school, free-time, holidays, etc.), play a fundamental role. Although they are not a guarantee that their children finally will result in the "optimal outcome" group, their presence significantly increases this possibility. Large-scale epidemiological studies should further clarify how strict and robust is the connection between parental engagement and the possibility of "optimal outcome".

Even if specific functional characteristics may limit neurocognitive and social skills improvement, one's own maximum potential should be considered for a positive result (that parental support and good treatments can foster). Thus, "optimal outcome resulting in functional recovery" should not be considered simplistically as "full recovery" from the diagnosis, also considering the fact that other neurodevelopmental comorbidities may persist (e.g., impacting attention, or language, or executive functions).

Optimal outcome: a new perspective

Finally, it is possible that a reconsideration of the construct of "optimal outcome" (or "optimal outcome resulting in functional recovery") is necessary on the basis of a further element: some scholars hypothesize that the focus on "optimal outcome" should be considered taking into account the recent view that tries to go beyond the one-directional idea that autism is a neurobiological disorder, and to promote the idea that autism is also the specific expression of a neurodiversity.

Indeed, it has been recently suggested that autism should be described as a neurodiversity.

Neurodiversity would frame autism as one of the declinations of human brain development, without any specific reference to any alleged standard or normal development. According to this framework, an individual with a diagnosis of ASD should not try to achieve an alleged standard level, but he/she should focus on person-based, well-balanced, and individualized outcomes that should maximize his/her socio-communicative and adaptive functioning.

At first glance, these two perspectives of autism (i.e., neurodevelopmental disorder versus neurodiversity) seem to be mutually exclusive and incompatible. However, both perspectives seem to agree in stating that autism is a condition with specific – although only marginally understood – neurobiological underpinnings.

The neurodiversity perspective de facto calls for a re-model of the constructs of "best outcome"/"optimal outcome"/"optimal outcome resulting in functional recovery" reported in the literature (that have been demonstrated to be useful to describe a specific – but numerically limited – subgroup of individuals). The neurodiversity perspective risks entailing just a partial understanding of the developmental trajectories that basically would be considered in their uniqueness and distinctiveness (neglecting the parts that contributed to identify a specific and "common" autistic core on which we ground the categorical diagnosis).

A strong emphasis on the neurodiversity perspective may risk of undermining the need of predisposing specific and ad hoc rehabilitative interventions (i.e., being just one of the several potential variants from the norm, why should we set specific clinical rehabilitation protocols?). Beyond this risk that should be taken into account to avoid negative cascade effects, maybe we should also consider that today autism is considered a dynamic and multilayered spectrum disorder (with age-dependent and context-dependent phenotypical manifestations), and in turn it needs a renovated definition of "outcome". From the one side, such a renovated view could establish a sort of synergy (or compromise) between the categorical approach (basically grounded on the phenotypical manifestations detected by standard clinical tests) and the neurodiversity approach (basically grounded on the functional diagnosis that takes into account the specific individual functioning).

To promote a perspective-shift in relation to the outcomes in the context of autism (e.g., how and when should we measure them) is probably desirable but – at the same time – we should recognize that this step is neither effortless nor easy. This change would in turn imply a significant reshaping of clinical services and supports for individuals with ASD and their families.

Most individuals with ASD need a series of clinical interventions that are tailored according to their specific evolution. Current longitudinal studies provide relevant support in describing variability of developmental trajectories; however, a major limitation concerns the fact that normally they do not take into account the impact of clinical services on developmental trajectories. Often their architecture does not permit to reply to such an urgent question. This limitation persists despite ASD scholars' wide recognition of the critical contribution of clinical service.

It happens that the architecture of certain longitudinal designs makes difficult the reply to this question; and this happens even if ascertaining when and how modifying rehabilitative protocols is crucial.

Future directions

One may consider three future steps for tackling these issues: first, to combine results of the first-wave prospective studies; second, to set new methods for approaching longitudinal experimental designs; and third, to develop clinical testing able to catch even subtle changes. There is a general consensus (even well-beyond the potential tension between the apparently conflicting views of autism as a disorder and autism as a neurodiversity) concerning the fact that the next crucial challenge for researchers will be to deal with the possibility to personalize clinical intervention according to the peculiar and fluctuant needs of individuals with ASD (and their families).

An additional further step will probably be to focus on rigorous monitoring of individuals with ASD showing better prognosis, supporting them during the transition to an independent life.

To date, research data and more generally the rigorous focus of research activities in the context of autism are more oriented to infancy and childhood; in contrast, the body of knowledge on autism in adulthood remains quite limited.

Available data seems to indicate that adults with ASD experience difficulties in certain crucial individual phases (e.g., job, friendship, sentimental relationships, etc.); in addition, a further factor concerns the limited attention to the peculiar subjective experience reported by adults with ASD, as if it does not matter how they feel the quality of their life.

This represents a concern also considering that, for example, young adults with ASD continuously compare their experience with that of their neurotypical peers (e.g., in terms of sentimental relationships, in terms of living independently). To some extent, they may feel that these opportunities are not expected for them.

Adults with ASD who have sharpened specific compensatory strategies and coping mechanisms to camouflage their difficulties in social interactions may be stressed by the effort of maintaining a sort of "mask" during social dynamics. Notably, additional distress can sometimes arise from the awareness that neurotypical individuals basically interact automatically without significant efforts, whereas they must put considerable effort in play.

Concerning standard quality of life indexes in adults with ASD, the literature seems to claim that only a limited part of them achieves positive values. There is a small amount of studies that try to clarify potential discrepancies between standard quality of life indexes and more condition-specific indexes (i.e., specifically designed for individuals with ASD). This interesting but numerically limited group of studies seem to suggest that ad hoc indexes for measuring quality of life in adults with ASD are more reliable.

There exists a critical gap between the current state of functioning and the desired state of functioning of individuals with ASD, as if they would face the gap between a "what is" and a "what can be". In turn, this further supports the idea that it can be promising to take into account peculiar, individualized, and nonstandard expectations concerning quality of life for each specific individual with ASD (influenced also by the context).

Accordingly, it is not enough to plan support according to standard areas of difficulties (e.g., socio-communicative); in contrast, it seems to be crucial to focus also on each individual's specific preferences, desires, and priorities. This should promote interventions that maximize the improvement of aspects that he/she considers as overriding.

Bibliography

Billstedt, E., Gillberg, I. C., & Gillberg, C. (2005). Autism after adolescence: Population-based 13- to 22-year follow-up study of 120 individuals with autism diagnosed in childhood. *Journal of Autism and Developmental Disorders*, 35(3), 351–360.

Bishop-Fitzpatrick, L., Hong, J., Smith, L. E., Makuch, R. A., Greenberg, J. S., & Mailick, M. R. (2016). Characterizing objective quality of life and normative outcomes in adults with autism spectrum disorder: An exploratory latent class analysis. *Journal of Autism and Developmental Disorders*, 46(8), 2707–2719.

Bishop-Fitzpatrick, L., Mazefsky, C. A., Minshew, N. J., & Eack, S. M. (2015). The relationship between stress and social functioning in adults with autism spectrum disorder and without intellectual disability. *Autism Research: Official Journal of the International Society for Autism Research*, 8(2), 164–173.

Cannon, J., O'Brien, A. M., Bungert, L., & Sinha, P. (2021). Prediction in autism spectrum disorder: A systematic review of empirical evidence. *Autism Research: Official Journal of the International Society for Autism Research*, 14(4), 604–630.

Cederlund, M., Hagberg, B., Billstedt, E., Gillberg, I. C., & Gillberg, C. (2008). Asperger syndrome and autism: A comparative longitudinal follow-up study more than 5 years after original diagnosis. *Journal of Autism and Developmental Disorders*, 38(1), 72–85.

Cohen, H., Amerine-Dickens, M., & Smith, T. (2006). Early intensive behavioral treatment: replication of the UCLA model in a community setting. *Journal of Developmental and Behavioral Pediatrics: JDBP*, 27(2 Suppl), S145–S155.

Courchesne, E., Karns, C. M., Davis, H. R., Ziccardi, R., Carper, R. A., Tigue, Z. D., Chisum, H. J., Moses, P., Pierce, K., Lord, C., Lincoln, A. J., Pizzo, S., Schreibman, L., Haas, R. H., Akshoomoff, N. A., & Courchesne, R. Y. (2001). Unusual brain growth patterns in early life in patients with autistic disorder: An MRI study. *Neurology*, 57(2), 245–254.

Cribb, S., Kenny, L., & Pellicano, E. (2019). 'I definitely feel more in control of my life': The perspectives of young autistic people and their parents on emerging adulthood. *Autism: The International Journal of Research and Practice*, 23(7), 1765–1781.

Dawson, G., Jones, E. J., Merkle, K., Venema, K., Lowy, R., Faja, S., Kamara, D., Murias, M., Greenson, J., Winter, J., Smith, M., Rogers, S. J., & Webb, S. J. (2012). Early behavioral intervention is associated with normalized brain activity in young children with autism. *Journal of the American Academy of Child and Adolescent Psychiatry*, 51(11), 1150–1159.

Eaves, L. C., & Ho, H. H. (2008). Young adult outcome of autism spectrum disorders. *Journal of Autism and Developmental Disorders*, 38(4), 739–747.

Eikeseth, S., Smith, T., Jahr, E., & Eldevik, S. (2007). Outcome for children with autism who began intensive behavioral treatment between ages 4 and 7: A comparison controlled study. *Behavior Modification*, 31(3), 264–278.

Fein, D., Barton, M., Eigsti, I. M., Kelley, E., Naigles, L., Schultz, R. T., Stevens, M., Helt, M., Orinstein, A., Rosenthal, M., Troyb, E., & Tyson, K. (2013). Optimal outcome in individuals with a history of autism. *Journal of Child Psychology and Psychiatry, and Allied Disciplines*, 54(2), 195–205.

Fein, D., Dixon, P., Paul, J., & Levin, H. (2005). Brief report: Pervasive developmental disorder can evolve into ADHD: Case illustrations. *Journal of Autism and Developmental Disorders*, 35(4), 525–534.

Fountain, C., Winter, A. S., & Bearman, P. S. (2012). Six developmental trajectories characterize children with autism. *Pediatrics*, 129(5), e1112–e1120.

Fountain, C., Winter, A. S., Cheslack-Postava, K., & Bearman, P. S. (2023). Developmental trajectories of autism. *Pediatrics*, 152(3), e2022058674.

Helt, M., Kelley, E., Kinsbourne, M., Pandey, J., Boorstein, H., Herbert, M., & Fein, D. (2008). Can children with autism recover? If so, how?. *Neuropsychology Review*, 18(4), 339–366.

Howlin, P., Goode, S., Hutton, J., & Rutter, M. (2004). Adult outcome for children with autism. *Journal of Child Psychology and Psychiatry, and Allied Disciplines*, 45(2), 212–229.

Kasari, C., Gulsrud, A., Freeman, S., Paparella, T., & Hellemann, G. (2012). Longitudinal follow-up of children with autism receiving targeted interventions on joint attention and play. *Journal of the American Academy of Child and Adolescent Psychiatry*, 51(5), 487–495.

Kelley, E., Paul, J. J., Fein, D., & Naigles, L. R. (2006). Residual language deficits in optimal outcome children with a history of autism. *Journal of Autism and Developmental Disorders*, 36(6), 807–828.

Khachadourian, V., Mahjani, B., Sandin, S., Kolevzon, A., Buxbaum, J. D., Reichenberg, A., & Janecka, M. (2023). Comorbidities in autism spectrum disorder and their etiologies. *Translational Psychiatry*, 13(1), 71.

Lord, C., Risi, S., Lambrecht, L., Cook, E. H., Jr, Leventhal, B. L., DiLavore, P. C., Pickles, A., & Rutter, M. (2000). The autism diagnostic observation schedule-generic: A standard measure of social and communication deficits associated with the spectrum of autism. *Journal of Autism and Developmental Disorders*, 30(3), 205–223.

Luyster, R., Richler, J., Risi, S., Hsu, W. L., Dawson, G., Bernier, R., Dunn, M., Hepburn, S., Hyman, S. L., McMahon, W. M., Goudie-Nice, J., Minshew, N., Rogers, S., Sigman, M., Spence, M. A., Goldberg, W. A., Tager-Flusberg, H., Volkmar, F. R., & Lord, C. (2005). Early regression in social communication in autism spectrum disorders: A CPEA study. *Developmental Neuropsychology*, 27(3), 311–336.

McCauley, J. B., Elias, R., & Lord, C. (2020). Trajectories of co-occurring psychopathology symptoms in autism from late childhood to adulthood. *Development and Psychopathology*, 32(4), 1287–1302.

Menezes, M., Robinson, M. F., Simmons, S. C., Smith, K. R., Zhong, N., & Mazurek, M. O. (2021). Relations among co-occurring psychopathology in youth with autism spectrum disorder, family resilience, and caregiver coping. *Research in Autism Spectrum Disorders*, 85, 101803.

Sallows, G. O., & Graupner, T. D. (2005). Intensive behavioral treatment for children with autism: Four-year outcome and predictors. *American Journal of Mental Retardation: AJMR*, 110(6), 417–438.

Saulnier, C. A., & Klin, A. (2007). Brief report: Social and communication abilities and disabilities in higher functioning individuals with autism and Asperger syndrome. *Journal of Autism and Developmental Disorders*, 37(4), 788–793.

Schendel, D. E., Overgaard, M., Christensen, J., Hjort, L., Jorgensen, M., Vestergaard, M., & Parner, E. T. (2016). Association of psychiatric and neurologic comorbidity with mortality among persons with autism spectrum disorder in a Danish population. *JAMA Pediatrics*, 170(3), 243–250.

Seltzer, M. M., Shattuck, P., Abbeduto, L., & Greenberg, J. S. (2004). Trajectory of development in adolescents and adults with autism. *Mental Retardation and Developmental Disabilities Research Reviews*, 10(4), 234–247.

Steinhausen, H. C., Mohr Jensen, C., & Lauritsen, M. B. (2016). A systematic review and meta-analysis of the long-term overall outcome of autism spectrum disorders in adolescence and adulthood. *Acta psychiatrica Scandinavica*, 133(6), 445–452.

Sutera, S., Pandey, J., Esser, E. L., Rosenthal, M. A., Wilson, L. B., Barton, M., Green, J., Hodgson, S., Robins, D. L., Dumont-Mathieu, T., & Fein, D. (2007). Predictors of optimal outcome in toddlers diagnosed with autism spectrum disorders. *Journal of Autism and Developmental Disorders*, 37(1), 98–107.

Turner, L. M., & Stone, W. L. (2007). Variability in outcome for children with an ASD diagnosis at age 2. *Journal of Child Psychology and Psychiatry, and Allied Disciplines*, 48(8), 793–802.

Watt, N., Wetherby, A. M., Barber, A., & Morgan, L. (2008). Repetitive and stereotyped behaviors in children with autism spectrum disorders in the second year of life. *Journal of Autism and Developmental Disorders*, 38(8), 1518–1533.

Woodman, A. C., Smith, L. E., Greenberg, J. S., & Mailick, M. R. (2015). Change in autism symptoms and maladaptive behaviors in adolescence and adulthood: the role of positive family processes. *Journal of Autism and Developmental Disorders*, 45(1), 111–126.

Conclusive Considerations

We started this book stating that the term "autism" raises a myriad of contrasting replies, feelings, reactions, and concerns. It is clear that we have not replied or solved all of them. Nevertheless, certain issues touched transversally in the five chapters can provide some significant insights for a deeper understanding of autism, and notably can contribute to outline the idea of autistic functioning.

A general framework raised from recent clinical and research advancements, and also sketched across the chapters, refers to the idea that autism has a sort of "double face". Autism is both a medical condition that needs specific clinical intervention and a form of neurodiversity that implies atypical profiles of functioning. The focus on heterogeneity and phenotypical instability of autism has been also crucial in this work. Heterogeneity of autism has been described across the chapters, deconstructing its multiple meanings. Instability of autistic behavioral manifestations has been considered in light of two main aspects: first, autism is an early emerging condition usually diagnosed in toddlerhood or childhood. In turn, this implies the need for considering individual development as a critical factor influencing changes in clinical manifestations. Second, autism is a neurodevelopmental condition that should be considered in light of peculiar derailments from the typical developmental course (i.e., atypical developmental trajectories). Thus, the *fil rouge* of this book can be summarized in three fundamental aspects that should orient any clinical practice (e.g., diagnosis, treatment, monitoring, etc.) in the context of autism: we need an *age*-dependent, *context*-dependent, and *functioning*-dependent approach. Noteworthy, these fundamental aspects should be attentively considered also in the research domain. Beyond the quite generic reference to biomarker discovery as basic framework to support research in the context of autism, we stressed the need of deconstructing the monolithic use of the term "biomarker". This should provide a refined and operationally more efficient way to deal with research data in the context of autism. Prudence, scientific and methodological robustness, and reliability are mandatory elements for any research endeavor. Benefiting from an age-, context-, and functioning-dependent approach to autism we should minimize the risk of neglecting one of the two "faces" of autism (i.e., medical condition and neurodiversity). In turn, this should limit the risk of confusing autistic and autistic-like manifestations, and should promote a deeper awareness concerning the fact that autistic-like phenotypical manifestations are not necessarily related to autism spectrum disorder (Chapter 2).

To support individuals with autism in pursuing their best feasible outcome is a matter of great importance for families, clinicians, educational services, caregivers, and, more generally, society. We should be all the main characters of this challenge.

Index

applied behavioral analysis (ABA) 63–4, 66–7, 69–73, 80, 86
atypical 1, 3, 9–10, 12, 15, 27, 29–30, 32, 34, 44–5, 49, 51–3, 62, 92, 94, 105–7, 120
autistic functioning 1–5, 7–12, 15, 22, 29–30, 36, 49–50, 120
autistic-like 29, 121

broader autism phenotype 49

caregivers 4–6, 8, 21, 28, 30–1, 43, 59, 72, 74, 76, 84–5, 94, 111, 121
cerebellum 28–9
comorbidity/comorbidities 5, 7, 64, 90, 92, 104, 109, 110, 113

deficit 12, 15–16, 22, 27, 62, 90, 112
development 3, 5–6, 26–9, 33, 42–4, 49, 51, 54–6, 58, 62–6, 70–5, 77, 79, 82–3, 85–90, 94, 104, 106, 109, 112–13, 120
diagnosis 1–3, 21–2, 25–7, 29–30, 42–53, 55–9, 63, 65, 91, 103, 105–10, 113, 120; categorical diagnosis 105, 107, 112, 114; differential diagnosis 7, 21, 23; early diagnosis 5, 106, 110; functional diagnosis 105, 107, 114
disability 1, 21–2, 24, 44, 46, 49, 106, 108

evidence-based 2, 4, 74

heterogeneity 8, 22–3, 120

intervention 4–5, 7, 16, 24–5, 30, 36, 46, 49, 57, 62–6, 70–9, 85–7, 91–3, 95–6, 103–4, 106, 109–10, 114–16, 120

longitudinal 114–15

marker/biomarker 7, 24–6, 30–7, 42, 51, 112, 121
medical 7, 21–2, 42, 51, 64, 91–2, 94, 96, 104–5, 107, 109–10, 120–1
multisensory 26–7, 29, 35–6

naturalistic 64, 69–72, 74, 77, 85
neurobiology/neurobiological 3, 21–3, 26, 29, 31, 46–7, 50, 51, 56, 62, 90, 107, 109, 110, 113
neurocognitive 25–30, 32, 34, 56, 63
neurodevelopment/neurodevelopmental 3, 5–7, 22–3, 29–30, 44, 55–6, 90, 106, 108, 113, 120
neurodiversity 22, 113–15, 120–1
neuroscience/neuroscientific 1–2, 14, 16–17, 21–37, 47
neurotypical 33–4, 53–6, 66, 85–6, 106, 108, 115

outcome 5, 45–6, 68, 83, 95, 104–6, 108–14, 121

phenotype/phenotypical 5–8, 15, 22–3, 25, 29–30, 44, 49, 51, 106–10, 112, 114, 120–1
prognosis 2, 26, 65, 103–5, 108–11, 115

recovery 104–10, 112–14
rehabilitation/rehabilitative 5, 7, 16, 22, 45, 47–8, 57, 62, 64, 91, 103–4, 106, 109–12, 114–15
reinforcement 64–6, 68, 70, 72–4, 78, 83, 86, 88
research/researcher 1–4, 6, 8, 10, 12, 15, 17, 22–5, 27, 29–31, 33, 36, 47, 76, 94, 96, 108, 115, 117, 120–1

sensory 6–7, 9–10, 18, 23, 26–30, 33, 35–6, 65, 84, 111; *see also* multisensory
social 1, 3, 6–7, 9, 12–18, 21, 23, 26–9, 33–4, 43, 48–9, 53, 56–7, 63–4, 71–90, 95, 106, 108, 110, 112–13, 115–16
spectrum 3–4, 27–9, 44, 46, 58–9, 62, 78, 114, 121

tailored 77, 80, 88, 93, 114
theory of mind 12–15, 17, 64
trajectory/trajectories 6, 26–7, 29, 44, 49, 51, 63, 71, 85, 103–6, 111–12, 114, 120
treatment 1–2, 4, 23–5, 47, 59, 62–3, 66, 70–3, 75–6, 78, 85–97, 103, 112–13, 120

Printed in the United States
by Baker & Taylor Publisher Services